For Orlando —
"Non furioso!"
Enjoy —
Devin
Kelly
Flying Sausages
5/96

Flying Sausages

SIMPLE, SAVORY RECIPES
FOR CREATING AND COOKING
WITH CHICKEN
AND TURKEY SAUSAGES

BY BRUCE AIDELLS AND DENIS KELLY

ILLUSTRATIONS BY STEVEN GUARNACCIA

CHRONICLE BOOKS
SAN FRANCISCO

ACKNOWLEDGMENTS

We'd like to thank the following friends and colleagues for recipes and advice:
Tom Blower, Marion Cunningham, Sue Farley, Margaret Fox and Chris Kumpf, Ken Hom, Haig Krikorian,
Bette Kroening, Marlene Levinson, Nancie McDermott, Nancy Oakes, Martha Perry, Claudia Roden, Amey Shaw, Julie and
Gary Wagner, Frances Wilson, and Edy Young. We are also grateful to Jacqueline Killeen, our editor, for her eagle eye
and unflagging attention to the task of good writing, and to our agent, Martha Casselman, for
her good sense and constant encouragement.

Library of Congress Cataloging-in-Publication Data:
Aidells, Bruce. Flying sausages: simple, savory recipes for creating and cooking with chicken and turkey sausages/
by Bruce Aidells and Denis Kelly: illustrations by Steven Guarnaccia.
p. cm. Includes index.
ISBN 0-8118-0541-7
1. Cookery (Sausages) 2. Sausages. I. Kelly, Denis, 1939-
II. Title. TX749.5.S28A367 1995
641.6 65 — dc20 94-19392 CIP
Printed in the United States of America.
Distributed in Canada by Raincoast Books, 8680 Cambie Street, Vancouver, B.C. V6P 6M9
10 9 8 7 6 5 4 3 2 1

CHRONICLE BOOKS
275 FIFTH STREET
SAN FRANCISCO, CA 94103

Contents

Introduction: Chicken and Turkey Sausages

In this book we'll provide you with quick and easy recipes for seven different types of sausage made from ground chicken and/or turkey. These master recipes embody the flavors of sausages from the American Midwest, Louisiana, the Southwest, Italy, the Mediterranean, China, and Thailand. The sausages are simple to make, don't have to be stuffed into casings, and can be wrapped and stored in the freezer for later use.

We then show you how to incorporate these tasty sausages into a great range of dishes that re-create the flavors of these seven cuisines — from spicy appetizers, snacks, and sandwiches to delicious breakfast dishes, salads, soups, pastas, main courses, and side dishes.

The technique is simple: Take a half-pound package or two of sausage out of the freezer, defrost it in the microwave if you're in a hurry, and use it to make a spicy pasta like our Capellini with Sausage, Lemon, and Basil; a tangy salad such as our Chinese Salad with Ginger Orange Dressing; or a satifying main dish like Creole Turkey Grillades.

You control the fat and salt levels and you decide what goes into your body (and your family's). You can enjoy yourself, eat food that is full of flavor, and not have to worry about it.

BRUCE SAYS:

"I STARTED MAKING SAUSAGE AND SELLING IT TO FRIENDS
IN RESTAURANTS ALL AROUND THE SAN FRANCISCO BAY AREA. WE ALL
HAD TASTED THESE FANTASTIC, SPICY SAUSAGES—ANDOUILLE,
CHAURICE, BOUDIN—IN EUROPE AND IN NEW ORLEANS. AND WE WANTED TO
USE THEM IN THE NEW STYLE OF COOKING THAT WAS EMERGING IN BERKELEY
IN THOSE DAYS. I USED JUST ENOUGH FAT TO MAKE THEM
JUICY, ONLY ENOUGH SALT FOR FLAVOR, LOTS OF SPICES, AND THE BEST MEAT
AVAILABLE. THE NEXT THING I KNEW THE PHONE WAS
RINGING OFF THE HOOK."

A few years back, creative sausage makers began to play with an idea—low-fat sausage. Fat has always been a part of sausage, which is really nothing more than ground meat, salt, and spices. Without natural fat from the meat, sausage would be dry as dust, lacking the juiciness and flavor we all love. But some commercial sausage makers carry the fat too far. Fat is cheaper than meat and mass-produced sausages sometimes end up containing up to 50 percent fat, far too high for health and optimum flavor. People began to be rightly concerned about the levels of fat, salt, and additives in their food.

DENIS SAYS:

"I WAS COOKING PART-TIME IN A CREOLE/CAJUN RESTAURANT, ROCK AND ROLL HONKYTONK, AND HOTBED OF RADICAL ACTIVITY IN THE EARLY 1970S WHEN I FIRST CAME ACROSS *BOUDIN* AND HOT LINKS. WE BOUGHT THEM FROM A SHOP IN THE OLD HOUSEWIVE'S MARKET IN OAKLAND—THE SAUSAGE MAKER HAD A PRETTY HEAVY HAND WITH THE HOT PEPPER, AND OUR CUSTOMERS LOVED THEM. THESE LINKS WEREN'T VERY SUBTLE (NEITHER WERE THE CUSTOMERS, NOW THAT I THINK OF IT), BUT THE HOT SAUSAGES SURE MADE YOU SIT UP AND TAKE NOTICE WHEN YOU BIT INTO THEM. THEY ALSO PROVOKED A PRODIGIOUS THIRST FOR DRAFT ANCHOR STEAM BEER, WHICH WAS THE PREFERRED LUBRICANT FOR POLITICAL DISCUSSION IN THOSE HEADY DAYS. BUT WHEN BRUCE'S ANDOUILLE CAME ON THE SCENE, IT WAS A REVELATION: THE SAUSAGE WAS NOT ONLY *HOT*—IT HAD REAL FLAVOR TOO!"

Then, artisan sausage makers started making high quality sausages with much lower levels of salt and fat than most commerical products. They used no additives other than the minimum of salt, and they aimed for around 25 percent fat in their sausages—about the level of ground chuck.

The products of these innovators met with great success, and their flavorful sausages became national favorites. But they wanted to reduce the fat even further and began to experiment with using chicken and turkey instead of pork and beef in their products. The challenge was to lower the fat content even more, and still obtain a juicy and flavorful result. The sausage makers replaced fat with savory ingredients such as apples, roasted peppers, sun-dried tomatoes, mushrooms, onions, cilantro, and other fresh herbs. The goal was to achieve a delicious sausage, yet keep the fat at around 10 to 12 percent, which is the normal amount contained in a chicken or turkey thigh.

"POULET WAS A COMBINATION DELICATESSEN AND RESTAURANT RIGHT IN THE
MIDDLE OF BERKELEY'S GOURMET GHETTO. WHEN I WAS CHEF THERE IN
THE LATE 1970S, THE TRICK WAS TO USE ONLY CHICKEN IN EVERYTHING WE
SERVED. SO THE PROGRESSION TO CHICKEN-BASED SAUSAGE WAS A NATURAL.
I TOOK THE IDEA OF LOW-FAT SAUSAGE ONE STEP FURTHER AND ADDED
CHOPPED APPLES, ONIONS, PEPPERS, AND OTHER NATURALLY JUICY
INGREDIENTS TO COMPENSATE FOR THE LOWER FAT LEVELS. AS I
EXPERIMENTED, MORE AND MORE CUSTOMERS LIKED THE CHICKEN AND APPLE
SAUSAGES AND THE ITALIAN DRIED TOMATO AND TURKEY SAUSAGES, SO
WHEN I STARTED AIDELLS SAUSAGE COMPANY I TRIED THESE PRODUCTS OUT
ON THE PUBLIC. THESE DAYS LOW-FAT, POULTRY-BASED SAUSAGES ARE
OUR MOST POPULAR CREATIONS AND WE'RE COMING UP WITH NEW VERSIONS
EVERY DAY."

New sausages like chicken and apple sausage and Italian turkey sausage with sun-dried tomatoes succeeded in providing plenty of taste and juiciness without high levels of fat. A plus was that these natural additives created flavor profiles that make these low-fat poultry sausages into "flavor bombs." Because the seasonings are already built into the sausage mixture, these chicken and turkey sausages enable you to incorporate the flavors of a cuisine or style of cooking into almost any dish with a minimum of preparation and without adding fat or excess calories.

"I DO A LOT OF THE COOKING AT HOME. SO WITH TWO COLLEGE-AGE KIDS
AND THEIR FRIENDS ARRIVING IN RANDOM TRIBELIKE SWIRLS AT TIMES,
IT'S NICE TO HAVE SOMETHING ON HAND THAT: A) IS EASY TO COOK, B) IS
CHEAP, C) DOESN'T CONTAIN RED MEAT, D) IS LOW IN FAT, AND E) IS INFI-
NITELY VARIABLE. THESE POULTRY-BASED SAUSAGES FIT THE BILL—THE KIDS
DESCEND IN DROVES NOW, AND OVER THE DINNER TABLE HAVE TAKEN TO
DEBATING EACH OTHER ABOUT THEIR FAVORITES. WE NOW HAVE A THAI
SAUSAGE FACTION VERSUS A SPICY LOUISIANA SAUSAGE FACTION, AND THE
KIDS OFTEN CALL FROM VARIOUS LOCALES BEFORE DINNER, INQUIRING WHAT
POULTRY SAUSAGES ARE ON THE MENU TONIGHT."

Poultry Sausages: Signatures of 7 Cuisines

Poultry Sausages: Signatures of 7 Cuisines

ausages have an uncanny ability to flavor even the blandest ingredients. All over the world sausage is used to add spice and excitement to virtually every kind of starch, staple, or vegetable you can think of. Rice, potatoes, beans, pasta, vegetables of all types gain new dimensions with the addition of sausage.

And just about every cuisine has its own sausage, its own flavor signature. From the lamb- and garlic-infused *merguez* of North Africa and the peppery Sicilian *salsicce* to the mild and aromatic American breakfast sausage and the sweet and savory Chinese *lop chong*, sausages are used in every way imaginable in soups, stews and salads, as snacks and pick-me-ups, as flavorings, and often as main courses in themselves. Our chicken and turkey sausages deliver all the flavor of these traditional sausages, but without the high fat and salt content of many commercial varieties.

Sausage has the added advantages of being quick and easy to use and is an inexpensive source of protein. Peasant cooks from northern Europe to Peking have always known that a bit of sausage can be fried up quickly to flavor large quantities of the everyday staple. Sausage often contains all the spice you need for rice or pasta, for example, and you don't have to spend a lot of time preparing and cooking other ingredients. And a little bit of sausage goes a very long way. Many of our recipes call for as little as one-half to one pound of spicy sausage to flavor a dish intended for four to six people.

The seven master recipes that follow will enable you to make the recipes in this book and many more besides. They are all based on chicken or turkey that you either grind yourself or can purchase preground from the supermarket. The sausage can be left in bulk and not stuffed into casings, although you can make sausage links if you prefer.

We suggest you make up master recipes for your favorite sausages, wrap them in plastic wrap or aluminum foil, and freeze them in half-pound packages for use in the recipes. Each batch provides enough sausage for seven or eight recipes. Making our sausages is not very complicated and does not require much in the way of equipment. A few hours on a Sunday afternoon are enough to stock your freezer with three or four batches of your favorite types.

You can take sausage out of the freezer the evening or morning before you want to use it, put it in the refrigerator, and take it out a half hour or so before you need it. Or if you are in a hurry, you can defrost sausage in the microwave; follow your microwave directions for defrosting hamburger. The sausage can still be a little frozen when you use it, since most recipes call for sautéing the sausage and breaking it apart as it cooks before adding other ingredients.

We do call for some exotic ingredients in our master recipes, especially for the Asian sausages. These are the authentic flavors of the regions, and you might be surprised at how available they are, especially in any city with a large Asian population. We describe these ingredients in our Glossary (page 220) and give you the names and addresses of mail-order purveyors in our Sources section (page 224).

We hope you'll be creative in using these tasty, low-fat sausages. They can be used in recipes from many traditions and styles of cooking from America, Europe, and Asia.

What about making the sausage? Isn't it time-consuming, messy, and hard to do? Don't you need a whole bunch of equipment? Don't you have to use pork, pork fat, and sausage casings to make good sausage? The answer to all these questions is no!

Because the sausage will be used in bulk form in most of our recipes, it doesn't have to go into a casing. This eliminates a lot of the work and makes the whole process much easier. All you really need to do is to grind or chop chicken or turkey thighs, blend in the spices, wrap the bulk sausage in half-pound packages, and refrigerate or freeze for later use. A food processor, meat grinder, or even a large sharp knife will get the job done nicely.

Also, if you are in hurry and don't want to grind your own, you can purchase preground chicken and/or turkey from the supermarket and simply blend in the spices. For best results, however, we recommend that you grind your own poultry, because you will then know that everything is impeccably fresh. But using preground chicken or turkey is an acceptable shortcut and turns out very tasty sausage with a minumum of time and fuss.

In any case, you should plan on making the sausage the day you buy the poultry or at least by the next day. And sausage that will not be consumed within a day or two should be frozen (it keeps up to three months in the freezer). Each of the batches makes about 3 1/2 to 4 pounds of sausage—enough for seven to eight recipes.

TO MAKE POULTRY SAUSAGE IN BULK

Remove the bone from chicken or turkey thighs, but leave the skin attached (unless otherwise specified). Our master sausage recipes call for net weights of boned chicken or turkey thighs, usually with skin, which provides extra flavor and juiciness. Bone weights average about 20 percent, so to end up with 3 1/2 pounds of boned chicken thighs with skin, you'll need about 4 1/2 pounds of unboned thighs (12 or so depending on size) to start with. Turkey thighs are more variable in size, but the 20 percent figure for bone weight can still be used. Dice the meat and skin into fairly uniform 1-inch pieces and put it into the freezer for 15 minutes. Add enough meat in a food processor just to cover the chopping blade (about 1 pound) and pulse to chop the meat into about 3/8-inch pieces. Remove the meat to a bowl as it is chopped and repeat in batches until all the meat is chopped. You may also grind the meat through a meat grinder using a 3/8-inch blade or chop the meat with a sharp knife into 3/8-inch pieces.

Put all the meat into a large bowl, add the ingredients called for in the recipe, and knead and stir the meat with your hands until everything is well blended. Do not overmix and warm up the sausage. Cover and refrigerate at once.

If you prefer to use preground chicken and/or turkey, chill the meat well and blend in the ingredients as directed.

To test that the spices and salt are to your liking, fry a small patty of the sausage for 2 to 3 minutes per side. Taste and add more salt or seasonings if you wish.

Wrap the bulk sausage into ½-pound packages using aluminum foil or plastic wrap, refrigerate, and use within 2 days, or freeze for up to 3 months.

A safety note: Make sure to wash well with hot water and soap all equipment and surfaces that come into contact with raw poultry.

TO MAKE LINK SAUSAGES

You will need a sausage horn attachment for your grinder or a sausage funnel. Wash the casings well in warm water to rinse out the salt and soak them for 1 or 2 hours. Attach the sausage horn to the grinder and remove the plate and knife. Pull the presoaked casing over the horn, leaving a few inches dangling at the end. Fill the grinder with ground sausage and feed it through the grinder until the meat begins to fill the casing. Tie the end of the casing into a knot and pierce any air bubbles that appear with a skewer or pin. Continue to feed the sausage into casings until all the sausage is used up. Casings should be full, but not overpacked or they will burst when you make the links. If you are using a sausage funnel, push the ground sausage through the funnel, following the preceding directions.

When a casing is full, form the links by pinching the casing at 5-inch intervals and twisting to seal links until the casing is fully linked. Knot the end of the casing and cut through the twisted casings to produce individual sausages. Refrigerate immediately and use within 2 days or freeze for up to 3 months.

If you live in an area that is fortunate enough to still have a real butcher that makes his own sausage, ask him if he will sell you some casings (we prefer medium hog casings). Otherwise, check the phone book under "butcher supplies" or "sausage casings." We also provide mail order sources for casings and sausage-making equipment (see Sources, page 224)

Chicken and Apple Sausage

American memories: sausage sputtering on the stove, waffles baking in an old-fashioned waffle iron, applesauce and maple syrup on the table, coffee steaming in a white enamel pot.

Country sausage has always been a mainstay in American cooking. It is part of the quintessential American breakfast, of course, but it has also been used as a flavoring by creative cooks from colonial times to the present. In New England, the Midwest, and the South, this savory mixture of pork, sage, black pepper, and spices is featured in a wide variety of dishes from Pennsylvania Dutch *schnitz und knepp* (a blend of sausage and apples) and scrapple (sausage mixed with cornmeal) to soups, stews, and casseroles of every type imaginable. Country sausage is also a wonderful flavoring for greens and other vegetables, providing an extra dimension of flavor and a hint of spice to otherwise bland ingredients.

We've taken the traditional country sausage recipe and lightened it up a bit by using chicken in place of pork, and by adding dried apples, cider, and sweet hints of cinnamon and ginger. The essential flavors are still there, but without the excess fat and cholesterol of earlier versions. You can use this mild and aromatic sausage wherever you want the characteristic flavors of American country sausage.

You can serve this sausage as a main course with a spicy sauce or relish, as in our Chicken and Apple Sausage with Onion Confit (page 148) or use it as a flavoring agent for vegetables, beans, or rice. We also use the rich and mildly sweet sausage in our Kids' Favorite Meat Loaf with Cider Gravy (page 175). We think Chicken and Apple Sausage is delicious as a stuffing for poultry, and even for fish. It is especially good in our Onion, Sausage, and Apple Stuffing (page 204).

Our section on breakfasts lists many uses for lightly spicy sausage including Sausage and Creamy Eggs in Popovers (page 66), and stuffed french toast (page 84) where fried patties are inserted between pieces of French toast and covered with sautéed apples and a syrup made from fresh apple cider.

While we think that all our sausages are delicious when left in bulk and frozen for use as patties or in recipes, our Chicken and Apple Sausage is one that you might also consider stuffing into links. This is not a particularly difficult process and can be the basis for a sausage-making party for family and friends. If you do decide to make links, you should prepare a double or triple recipe to provide enough sausage for many delicious breakfasts to come.

1 cup apple cider

3 1/2 pounds boned chicken thighs with skin (about 4 1/2
   pounds with bones) or 3 1/2 pounds ground chicken

3 ounces dried apples

4 teaspoons kosher salt

2 teaspoons freshly ground black pepper

2 teaspoons dried sage

1/8 teaspoon ground cinnamon

1/8 teaspoon ground nutmeg

1/4 teaspoon ground ginger

1 chicken bouillon cube dissolved in 2 tablespoons
   boiling water

8 to 10 feet medium sausage casings (optional)

In a small nonreactive saucepan, boil down the cider almost to a syrup, about 2 to 3 tablespoons. Cool and reserve.

If using chicken thighs, coarsely grind the boned chicken and skin or chop coarsely in batches in a food processor (see To Make Poultry Sausage in Bulk, page 14).

Add the apple cider and the remaining ingredients to the ground chicken in a large bowl or plastic tub and blend thoroughly with your hands. Fry a small patty until done and taste for salt, pepper, and other seasonings.

Divide the sausage into 7 or 8 portions (each about 1/2 pound), wrap tightly in plastic wrap or aluminum foil, and refrigerate or freeze for later use. Or, if desired, stuff the sausage into casings (see To Make Link Sausages, page 15).

Makes seven or eight 1/2-pound packages or about twenty 5-inch link sausages.

SUBSTITUTIONS FOR CHICKEN AND APPLE SAUSAGE

Chicken and apple sausages are available around the country in better grocery stores and butcher shops and from mail-order sources (page 224). Or use good quality American sage and pepper sausage, add some chopped dried apples, and drain off fat before using.

Spicy Louisiana Sausage

When the fiddles tune up, the accordions start to wheeze, and the triangle begins to beat out a lively two-step, you know the party is about to get going down in Cajun country. Along with the music and dance and Dixie beer, you are sure to partake of substantial amounts of some of the hottest and most flavorful cooking anywhere.

In the rollicking city of New Orleans and along the bayous and prairies of southern Louisiana, a style of cooking was created that is one of the glories of American cuisine. Creole chefs in the big city and Cajun cooks in the countryside drew on Native American, African, French, Spanish, and Caribbean traditions to create a vibrant cuisine filled with spice and seafood, a style of cooking with rich and hearty flavors that are tied to the earth and the great river delta that feeds the region.

Gumbos made from peppers, okra, hot sausage, chicken, game, or seafood, often seasoned with filé (a blend of thyme and native sassafras bark), are a prime example of this earthy mixture of foods and cultures. American and European ingredients blend with African (*n'gombo* is the West African word for "okra") in these succulent soup/stews. Gumbos are great one-dish meals, which don't have to be high in fat or calories. Our Eggplant Gumbo (page 96) made with our version of the spicy Louisiana sausage, *chaurice*, is a lively and flavorful rendition of this Louisiana favorite.

Our Spicy Louisiana Sausage is found in peppery New Orleans specialities such as our Creole Corn and Seafood Chowder (page 95), Creole Turkey Grillades (page 169), and Louisiana Po'Boy with Creole Mustard Sauce (page 60).

We suggest you use this sausage wherever you want a slightly smoky, decidedly spicy note. It can dress up beans, pasta, salads, and vegetables by adding lots of flavor without excessive amounts of fat or cholesterol.

2 cups sliced onions
1 1/2 pounds boned chicken thighs without skin (about
   2 pounds with bones) or 1 1/2 pounds ground chicken
1 1/2 pounds boned turkey thighs without skin (about
   2 pounds with bones) or 1 1/2 pounds ground turkey
1/2 pound bacon, cut into pieces
1 1/2 tablespoons chopped garlic
2 teaspoons dried thyme
1 teaspoon dried sage
1 teaspoon dried oregano

1 teaspoon red pepper flakes
1/2 teaspoon ground allspice
1 teaspoon English-style dry mustard
2 teaspoons yellow mustard seed
1 teaspoon sugar
1 teaspoon cayenne pepper
1/4 cup paprika
4 teaspoons kosher salt
1 tablespoon freshly ground black pepper

Simmer the onions in water to cover until translucent, 5 to 7 minutes. Cool under cold running water and drain. (Make sure onions are cool. They can be made ahead of time and refrigerated for later use.) Coarsely grind the onions with the chicken, turkey, and bacon or chop coarsely in batches in a food processor (see To Make Poultry Sausage in Bulk, page 14). If using previously ground chicken or turkey, coarsely grind or chop the onions and bacon and mix thoroughly with the ground poultry.

Add the remaining ingredients to the ground meat mixture in a large bowl or plastic tub and blend thoroughly with your hands. Fry a small patty until done and taste for salt, pepper and other seasonings.

Divide the sausage into 7 or 8 portions (each about 1/2 pound), wrap tightly in plastic wrap or aluminum foil, and refrigerate or freeze for later use.

Makes seven or eight 1/2-pound packages.

SUBSTITUTIONS FOR SPICY LOUISIANA SAUSAGE

Louisiana *chaurice*, andouille, and other hot Louisiana-style sausages are available from mail-order sources (page 224). Or use good quality hot sage and pepper sausage, add some red pepper flakes, cook, and drain off fat before using. You could also use some hot Italian pork or turkey sausage and mix in a little sage (about 1/2 teaspoon per pound).

Southwest Green Chile Sausage

On the outskirts of Albuquerque, there's a tiny taco joint that you come across after a long drive through the harsh and beautiful high desert. The owner makes his own chorizo, the tortillas are handmade and grilled to order, and the old-fashioned cooler is full of ice-cold Bohemia and Carta Blanca. It's a natural place to pause after a long day's journey.

We've eaten just about everything on the menu over the past few years of travel and tasting, and we keep coming back to the same dish again and again—chopped chicken with green chiles. This spicy hash is made from real barnyard chickens (you can see them scratching in the dust outside) and chiles from the garden in back. The chicken and green chile mixture is used to stuff tacos, burritos, and tamales, and it is typical of the hearty and healthy food found throughout the Southwest.

Southwestern cooking is based on the Mexican staples of pork, chicken, chiles, corn, and beans and is suddenly the rage in popular eateries from L.A. to New York. Many chefs are creating exciting new dishes based on this spicy and earthy style of cooking, combining traditional ingredients in new and unusual ways.

One way to incorporate the flavors of the Southwest into your cooking is by using sausage. Chorizo—ground beef or pork combined with chiles, wine, and vinegar—adds plenty of flavor, but most commercial versions are a bit greasy. We've created a lighter chicken and turkey sausage using jalapeños and fire-roasted Anaheim chiles blended with garlic, cumin, and cilantro along with some dark beer and an optional belt of tequila. You can use it in place of chorizo or (just like our friend outside Albuquerque) in tacos, burritos and tamales.

This sausage makes a great taco: Just fry some up in a little vegetable oil, put a couple of tablespoons of the cooked sausage into a heated tortilla, along with a healthy dollop of Salsa Cruda (page 213), some Guacamole (page 211), and some of our Lime Pickled Onions (page 214). Pop open a bottle of Dos Equis and fall to.

The spicy sausage adds life to salads such as our Southwest Black Bean Salad (page 114) and Southwest Green Chile Sausage and Cabbage Salad (page 115) and makes mouthwatering appetizers such as Lalime's Southwest Green Chile Burrito (page 40). It may also be used as a main course when formed into patties and grilled or blended into our Southwest Meat Loaf (page 177).

FIRE-ROASTING GREEN CHILES OR BELL PEPPERS

Care should be taken in handling chiles; use rubber gloves or wash your hands thoroughly after touching hot chiles.

To fire-roast green chiles or bell peppers, char the peppers over an open flame or under a hot broiler, place in a plastic bag for 10 to 15 minutes to sweat, and then scrape off the skin and seeds. Ortega brand canned fire-roasted green chiles are an acceptable substitute for fresh mild chiles.

1¾ *pounds boned chicken thighs with skin (about*
  2¼ pounds with bones) or 1¾ pounds ground chicken
1¾ *pounds boned turkey thighs with skin (about*
  2¼ pounds with bones) or 1¾ pounds ground turkey
1 jalapeño chile,* seeded, deveined, and finely chopped
  (1 to 2 tablespoons)
2 teaspoons ground cumin
Pinch ground cinnamon
⅓ *cup pure New Mexican chile powder**

½ *tablespoon freshly ground black pepper*
½ *teaspoon cayenne pepper*
1½ *tablespoons kosher salt*
¼ *cup amber beer (such as Dos Equis)*
2 tablespoons tequila (optional)
1 Anaheim chile,* fire-roasted (page 20), seeded,
  deveined, and chopped
1 bunch (4 to 6 ounces) cilantro, chopped (about 1 cup)
* *See Glossary*

If using chicken and turkey thighs, coarsely grind the meat and skin or chop coarsely in batches in a food processor (see To Make Poultry Sausage in Bulk, page 14).

Add the remaining ingredients to the ground chicken and turkey in a large bowl or plastic tub and blend thoroughly with your hands. Fry a small patty until done and taste for salt, pepper, and other seasonings.

Divide the sausage into 7 or 8 portions (each about a ½ pound), wrap tightly in plastic wrap or aluminum foil, and refrigerate or freeze for later use.

Makes seven or eight ½-pound packages.

SUBSTITUTIONS FOR SOUTHWEST GREEN CHILE SAUSAGE

Southwest-style poultry sausages are available around the country in better grocery stores and butcher shops and from mail-order sources (page 224). Or use good quality chorizo, add some chopped green chiles, cook, and drain off fat before using.

Italian Turkey and Sun-Dried Tomato Sausage

I taly, from the Alps to Sicily, is a mosaic of flavors and tastes. Each region has its own style of cooking: the tomatoes and garlic of the south, earthy mushrooms and truffles in Piedmont, spaghetti with garlic and oil in Rome's Trastevere, spicy seafood along the Ligurian coast, rich cheese and succulent prosciutto in Emilia-Romagna, beans and fragrant green olive oil in Tuscany.

And each of these regions and styles of cooking has its own particular style of sausage. Some, especially in the north, are flavored with aromatic spices and herbs; others are fragrant with garlic and wine; while fennel, sun-dried tomatoes, cheese, red pepper, and other pungent additions are favorite flavors in Naples and the south.

We've put together a delicious sausage that blends sun-dried tomatoes, wine, fennel, red pepper, and lots of garlic with turkey as a base. You can vary the recipe a bit for regional character—more garlic and red pepper for a Calabrese touch, for example, or even more garlic along with a couple of tablespoons of Romano cheese for a hint of the south. Use this savory sausage wherever you want an Italian accent. It's perfect for pasta, especially when combined with fresh tomatoes, garlic, and basil.

Delicious and easy-to-make pasta dishes using this sausage include Capellini with Sausage, Lemon and Basil (page 133), Linguine with Italian Sausage and Arugula (page 137), and Spaghettini with Sausage, Anchovies, and Bread Crumbs (page 139).

This aromatic sausage also combines wonderfully with cheese in our Baked Penne with Sausage, Sun-Dried Tomatoes, and Ricotta (page 134) and our Cheese and Sausage Ravioli with Fresh Tomato and Basil Sauce (page 144). It is, of course, a natural topping for pizza (Quick Pizza, page 158), and can be used to spice up beans (Pasta with Sausage and Beans, page 135, and Tuscan Bean Soup, page 101), polenta (Smoked Cheese Polenta with Sun-Dried Tomatoes, page 195), salads (Italian Sausage and Spinach Salad with Polenta Croutons, page 116) and appetizers (Crostini with Tomato and Sausage Topping, page 32).

....

3¹/₂ pounds boned turkey thighs with skin (about 4¹/₂
*   pounds with bones) or 3¹/₂ pounds ground turkey*
3 tablespoons chopped garlic
¹/₃ cup chopped sun-dried tomatoes packed in olive oil*
¹/₄ cup white wine
2 tablespoons fennel seed

1 teaspoon red pepper flakes
4 teaspoons kosher salt
1 tablespoon freshly ground black pepper
1 teaspoon sugar

* See Glossary

....

If using turkey thighs, coarsely grind the boned turkey and skin, or chop coarsely in batches in a food processor (see To Make Poultry Sausage in Bulk, page 14).

Add the remaining ingredients to the ground turkey in a large bowl or plastic tub and blend thoroughly with your hands. Fry a small patty until done and taste for salt, pepper, and other seasonings.

Divide the sausage into 7 or 8 portions (each about $\frac{1}{2}$ pound), wrap tightly in plastic wrap or aluminum foil, and refrigerate or freeze for later use.

Makes seven or eight $\frac{1}{2}$-pound packages.

SUBSTITUTIONS FOR ITALIAN TURKEY AND SUN-DRIED TOMATO SAUSAGE

Poultry-based Italian sausages are available around the country in better grocery stores and butcher shops and from mail-order sources (page 224). Or use good quality sweet Italian sausage and add chopped sun-dried tomatoes.

LOW-FAT COOKING

Our recipes keep fat to a minimum needed for flavor, and most recipes using our low-fat sausage suggest that it be browned in a little oil before adding to the dish. If you really want the fat levels low, you can brown the sausage in a nonstick pan without adding oil, and then drain off and discard any fat remaining. You'll lose some flavor, but if you are a fanatic about cutting the calories that's the way to do it. For salads and pastas where the oil is part of the dressing or sauce, you should use at least half the oil and not drain off the pan juices. A good way to remove fat from soups, sauces, and stews is to blot it up by laying a paper towel briefly on top and then removing the towel with the fat it has soaked up. Use as many pieces of paper towel as you need until all the fat is gone.

Mediterranean Sausage

I t's early evening, the sun just gone down into the Mediterranean. Fishing boats chug out of the harbor, their lanterns glowing in the fading light. You're sitting on the terrace of your favorite cafe, sipping arrak or ouzo, fino sherry or mint tea, nibbling on a plate of spicy snacks, with *bazoukis* or ouds or guitars wailing away in the background. On the table are crisp fried calamari, salty olives, a sharp cheese, yogurt and garlic mixed in a bowl with mint leaves. And suddenly you bite down on a crunchy sausage full of garlic and pepper, lemon, cumin, mint, coriander—the flavors of the Mediterranean from Tangiers to the Piraeus, Siracusa to Alexandria.

In this part of the world, garlic is used everywhere in just about everything: in tangy sauces based on yogurt (*tzaziki*), blended with chickpeas (hummus) or sesame (tahini), in sautés of tomatoes and seafood. Peppers— red, green, and golden—give Mediterranean cooking much of its life and zest. Lemons add piquancy to soups (*avgolemono*), long baked stews (*tagines*), vegetables and salads. Pungent spices, such as cumin and coriander, and aromatic herbs, like mint and oregano, provide an unmistakable undertone to many dishes.

All around the shores of the Mediterranean we find spicy, garlicky sausages made from pork and, in Arabic countries, lamb or beef. *Merguez* from Algeria, *loukanika* from Greece, and *shawarma* from Lebanon are all redolent of the flavors of the Middle East and are used to spice up lentils, chickpeas, rice, beans, and pasta. These tasty mixtures of meat and spices are often used to stuff vegetables, grape leaves, and pastries as appetizers (see our Mediterranean Sausage and Spinach Turnovers, page 44). Grilled sausages are especially delicious stuffed into pita bread with a piquant sauce (see our Pita with Mediterranean Sausage and Greek Caper Sauce, page 57).

We've lightened the sausage mix by using chicken and turkey, but the zesty flavors of the Mediterranean are still there. We love this aromatic sausage with lentils or pasta in a salad (see Marlene's Mediterranean Lentil Salad, page 120, and Mediterranean Orzo Salad, page 119). Mediterranean Sausage is delicious in soup with spinach or other greens in our Middle Eastern Spinach and Meatball Soup (page 105), with lamb in our Greek Braised Lamb Shanks (page 171), and in our savory Greek Sausage and Eggplant Stew (page 172). The sausage also adds an exotic note to fish and seafood in our West L.A. Persian Seafood Stew (page 150) and Swordfish Sicilian Style (page 149).

2 cups sliced onions

1 3/4 pounds boned chicken thighs with skin (about
   2 1/4 pounds with bones) or 1 3/4 pounds ground chicken

1 3/4 pounds boned turkey thighs, with skin (about
   2 1/4 pounds with bones) or 1 3/4 pounds ground turkey

1 tablespoon tomato paste

2 tablespoons chopped garlic

2 teaspoons fennel seed, ground in a mortar, spice grinder,
   or food processor

2 teaspoons ground cumin

2 teaspoons ground coriander

1/2 teaspoon ground allspice

1 teaspoon ground turmeric

2 tablespoons paprika

1/2 teaspoon cayenne pepper

2 teaspoons freshly ground black pepper

2 tablespoons kosher salt

1 teaspoon sugar

2 teaspoons finely chopped lemon zest

1 tablespoon fresh lemon juice

2 tablespoons olive oil

2 tablespoons chopped fresh mint or 2 teaspoons dried mint

1/4 cup chopped fresh Italian flat-leaf parsley

Simmer the onions in water to cover until translucent, 5 to 7 minutes. Cool under cold running water and drain. Coarsely grind the onions with the chicken, turkey, and skin or chop coarsely in batches in a food processor (see To Make Poultry Sausage in Bulk, page 14). If using previously ground chicken or turkey, omit this step, simmer and cool the onions, coarsely grind or chop them, and mix them thoroughly with the ground poultry.

Add the remaining ingredients to the ground poultry mixture in a large bowl or plastic tub and blend thoroughly with your hands. Fry a small patty until done and taste for salt, pepper, and other seasonings.

Divide the sausages into 7 or 8 portions (about 1/2 pound each), wrap tightly in plastic wrap or aluminum foil, and refrigerate or freeze for later use.

Makes seven or eight 1/2-pound packages.

SUBSTITUTIONS FOR MEDITERRANEAN SAUSAGE

Use good quality hot Italian sausage, preferably turkey based; add extra garlic and a pinch of curry powder.

Chinese Black Mushroom Sausage

Chinese cooks have created a rich and complex cuisine that has been a constant source of flavor and innovation in American cooking. An obsession with fresh, high quality ingredients, the ability to balance flavors with skill and imagination, and the subtle use of aromatics and spices are qualities that make Chinese cooking so satisfying. A plus is the Chinese attitude about meat and fat—most dishes use only enough meat to flavor large amounts of rice, noodles, or vegetables. Meat is seen as a condiment, rather than the main component of the meal.

This is why sausage works so well in Chinese-influenced food. Sausages are highly seasoned bits of meat which provide an explosion of flavor in bland ingredients, with a minimum of fat or calories. And if you use our recipes based only on chicken and turkey, even less fat and cholesterol are added to the dish.

Sausage is especially adaptable to stir-frying, where vegetables, meat or poultry, and flavorings are quickly cooked together and then served with rice or noodles (see our Chinese Sausage and Vegetable Stir-Fry, page 193, and Singapore Noodles with Black Mushroom Sausage, page 132). This quick and healthful method of cooking need not be limited to Asian dishes. It works just as well with a sauce for pasta or a quick sauté of fresh vegetables.

Chinese cooks frequently use the sweet, aromatic sausage *lop chong* in stir-fries and casseroles and stuff wontons and dim sum with highly seasoned mixtures of ground meat and seafood. We've adapted these techniques in recipes like Pot Stickers Filled with Chinese Black Mushroom Sausage (page 52), and Chinese Stuffed Mushrooms (page 53). With the availability of premade wrappers, dim sum, wontons, and even ravioli (page 144) are easy to make.

Much of the flavor excitement in Chinese dishes comes from aromatics, herbs, mushrooms, and spices. Our sausage incorporates smoky dried black mushrooms, fragrant sesame oil and soy, along with ginger, garlic, and sherry. Five spice powder—an aromatic blend of anise seed, fennel, clove, cinnamon, and cassia—gives an intriguing undertone.

We think this sausage adds a lot to salads and snacks, such as our Chinese Salad with Ginger Orange Dressing (page 125) and Chinese Sausage Sandwich with Hoisin Onions (page 61). It is also delicious as a main course in Edy's Chinese Stuffed Fish (page 152) and Ken Hom's Mo Shu with Chinese Black Mushroom Sausage (page 186).

HOW TO RECONSTITUTE DRIED MUSHROOMS

Place mushrooms in a heatproof glass bowl or large measuring cup. Cover with boiling water and soak for at least 30 minutes or up to 3 hours. Remove the mushrooms with a slotted spoon; then remove, discard tough stems, and reserve the caps. (Decant the soaking water off the gritty sediment to use later in soups, to cook rice, or for stir-frying.)

1 ³/₄ pounds boned chicken thighs with skin (about
   2 ¹/₄ pounds with bones) or 1 ³/₄ pounds ground chicken
1 ³/₄ pounds boned turkey thighs with skin (about
   2 ¹/₄ pounds with bones) or 1 ³/₄ pounds ground turkey
1 ounce Chinese dried black mushrooms* (10 to 12),
   reconstituted (page 26)
1 tablespoon Asian sesame oil*
¹/₄ cup Chinese dark soy sauce*
1 tablespoon chopped garlic

2 tablespoons chopped fresh ginger
¹/₂ cup finely chopped green onions, green and white parts
1 teaspoon chopped Chinese fermented black beans*
1 teaspoon five spice powder*
1 tablespoon kosher salt
1 tablespoon freshly ground black pepper
1 teaspoon sugar
2 tablespoons sweet sherry
* See Glossary

Coarsely grind the chicken, turkey, skin, and soaked black mushroom caps or chop coarsely in batches in a food processor (see To Make Poultry Sausage in Bulk, page 14). If using previously ground chicken or turkey, chop the black mushrooms and mix with the ground poultry.

Add the remaining ingredients to the poultry mixture in a large bowl or plastic tub and blend thoroughly with your hands. Fry a small patty until done and taste for salt, pepper, and other seasonings.

Divide the sausage into 7 or 8 portions (each about ¹/₂ pound each), wrap tightly in plastic wrap or aluminum foil, and refrigerate or freeze for later use.

Makes seven or eight ¹/₂-pound packages.

SUBSTITUTIONS FOR CHINESE BLACK MUSHROOM SAUSAGE

Use ground turkey, chicken, and/or pork and add seasonings in recipe.

Thai Chicken and Turkey Sausage

When people get their first taste of Thai cooking, it's often a revelation and they are converts for life. It's not exactly a bolt of lightning or a mystical experience, but rather the sudden thought "Why doesn't all food taste like this—fiery and bright and exciting?"

Thai food can become an obsession. It is so addictive that it can make you a little crazy. You stop strangers on the street and tell them about the squid salad you just ate. Breathing garlic, lemongrass, and mint in their terrified faces, you hold them by the lapel as they try to pull away, run after them waving your arms as they bolt through the traffic because you forgot to mention this fantastic green curry in the restaurant down the block.

Green chiles and lots of heat, fresh basil, mint and cilantro, limes and lemongrass, ginger, green curry, coconut milk, fish sauce—all these flavors make you want to sit up and sing (or at least reach for a Singha beer).

Our Thai Chicken and Turkey Sausage incorporates these flavors and gives you the ability to make delicious Thai-accented dishes easily and quickly. Taste-awakening appetizers such as our Savory Thai Seafood and Sausage Dumplings (page 47), Thai Sausage Satay (page 45) and Tiger Prawns Stuffed with Asian Sausage (page 49) are all made even more appealing with Nancy's Asian Dipping Sauce (page 48), a spicy mix of chiles, rice vinegar, limes, and fish sauce. The sausage is delightful in salads like our Thai Sausage Salad (page 124) and is especially good in our light and spicy Thai Sausage Soup (page 109). One of the most satisfying and flavorful Thai dishes is green curry made with a mixture of green chiles, Asian spices, fresh basil and lemongrass cooked with sausage and chicken (see Thai Green Curry, page 184, and Green Curry Paste, page 185).

As in other sausages, we use authentic Thai seasonings to give you the real flavors of the cuisine. We discuss these ingredients in our Glossary (page 220) and supply mail-order sources for them (page 224). The advantage is that you can incorporate these exotic flavors into 1/2-pound packages of sausage stored in the freezer, and you don't have to worry about keeping all the sauces and herbs on the shelf or in the pantry indefinitely.

ABOUT SALT

Salt is a necessary component of sausage's flavor and texture. If you use too little salt or leave it out altogether, the sausage will taste flat and bland. Salt is also necessary to stabilize the muscle proteins that act as a glue to bind the individual particles of meat together—without it the sausage would be crumbly and dry. Our recipes use a minimum of salt for flavor and binding, far less than most commercial products.

1 ³/₄ pounds boned chicken thighs with skin (about
   2 ¼ pounds with bones) or 1 ³/₄ pounds ground chicken
1 ³/₄ pounds boned turkey thighs with skin (about
   2 ¼ pounds with bones) or 1 ³/₄ pounds ground turkey
1 to 2 tablespoons Thai Green Curry Paste*, imported or
   homemade (page 185)
1 bunch (4 to 6 ounces) fresh cilantro, including stems and
   roots, cleaned and chopped (about 1 cup)
3 tablespoons chopped fresh basil

3 tablespoons chopped fresh mint
1 ½ tablespoons chopped garlic
1 ½ tablespoons chopped fresh ginger
¼ cup Southeast Asian fish sauce*
1 tablespoon kosher salt
1 teaspoon red pepper flakes
1 tablespoon freshly ground black pepper
1 teaspoon cayenne pepper

* See Glossary

If using chicken and turkey thighs, coarsely grind the meat and skin or chop coarsely in batches in a food processor (see To Make Poultry Sausage in Bulk, page 14).

Add the remaining ingredients to the ground chicken and turkey in a large bowl or plastic tub and blend thoroughly with your hands. Fry a small patty until done and taste for salt, pepper, and other seasonings.

Divide the sausage into 7 or 8 portions (about ½ pound each), wrap tightly in plastic wrap or aluminum foil, and refrigerate or freeze for later use.

Makes seven or eight ½-pound packages.

SUBSTITUTIONS FOR THAI CHICKEN AND TURKEY SAUSAGE

Thai-style sausages are available on the West Coast in better grocery stores and butcher shops and from mail-order sources (page 224). Or use ground turkey, chicken, and/or pork and add seasonings in recipe.

Appetizers, Snacks, and Sandwiches

Appetizers, Snacks, and Sandwiches

With a few packages of our chicken or turkey sausages in the freezer, you'll never have to worry about an impromptu party or the last-minute arrival of unexpected guests. Each sausage is packed with flavor. With some condiments and a little imagination, you can put together a party without a lot of fuss and with very little lead time.

But our sausages are not only good for parties, planned or unplanned. They also make tasty and interesting appetizers or first courses which will perk up the taste buds of your friends and family. Chinese Stuffed Mushrooms (page 53) and Pot Stickers Filled with Chinese Black Mushroom Sausage (page 52) make a great beginning to a Chinese banquet. Thai Sausage Satay (page 45), Tiger Prawns Stuffed with Asian Sausage (page 49), Savory Thai Seafood and Sausage Dumplings (page 47), or Korean Green Onion and Sausage Cakes (page 50) are delicious starters to an Asian meal or provide the basis for an exotic appetizer party.

An Italian feast beginning with an assortment of crostini (page 32) will remind you of fine meals served in Tuscany. And if you just want to give your guests' palates a spicy wake-up call, serve our Mediterranean Sausage and Spinach Turnovers (page 44), Spicy Meatballs Braised with Beer and Onions (page 34), or Lalime's Southwest Green Chile Burrito (page 40).

Crostini with Tomato and Sausage Topping

Crostini are small rounds of toasted Italian bread, sprinkled with olive oil and rubbed with garlic, topped with a spicy bit of sausage or olive paste or, more elaborately, spread with a pâté of chicken livers garnished with shaved white truffles. Crostini are especially popular in Tuscany, where they are often part of an antipasto platter. They also make delicious appetizers with a dry white wine such as Tuscan Galestro or California Sauvignon Blanc. And crostini may also serve as an appetizing first course on a bed of dressed greens such as mesclun, arugula, and/or radicchio. Our version features Fresh Tomato Vinaigrette spooned on toasted bread that is topped with a small slice or patty of grilled Italian sausage. But use your own imagination in making crostini. They are easy to prepare, delicious, and endlessly variable.

1 baguette (about 25 inches) or other French or Italian bread
½ cup olive oil
Salt as needed

1 pound Italian Turkey and Sun-Dried Tomato Sausage (page 22), shaped into forty 2-inch patties, or 4 to 5 links of Italian sausage
Fresh Tomato Vinaigrette (following)

Preheat the oven to 375°F. Cut the bread into forty ½-inch rounds. Brush each slice with olive oil and sprinkle lightly with salt. Arrange the slices on a baking sheet and bake until the toasts are golden brown and crisp, about 20 minutes. Cool briefly and use at once.

In a large skillet, panfry patties or whole links until lightly browned and cooked through (5 to 7 minutes for patties, turning once or twice; about 10 minutes for whole sausages, turning often). If using bulk sausage, remove patties from the pan and keep warm. If using links, slice each link into about 10 slices to make a total of 40 slices. Spoon some of the tomato vinaigrette onto each toast round and top with a patty or a slice of sausage. Place crostini on a platter and serve immediately.

Makes 40 crostini, serves 6 to 8 as antipasto or 4 or 5 as part of a first-course salad on a bed of greens.

Fresh Tomato Vinaigrette

....

This simple vinaigrette is also delicious on cooled pasta or tossed with greens, sliced cooked new potatoes, and quartered hard-cooked eggs. Combined with roasted eggplant, it serves as a basis for a condiment to serve with our Italian Super Hero (page 56).

³/₄ cup finely chopped ripe tomatoes
3 tablespoons balsamic or raspberry vinegar
3 tablespoons chopped fresh basil
2 anchovy fillets, chopped
¹/₄ cup freshly grated Parmesan cheese

2 sun-dried tomatoes packed in olive oil,* finely chopped
¹/₃ cup extra-virgin olive oil
Salt and freshly ground black pepper to taste

* See Glossary

In a small bowl, mix together all the ingredients except the oil and salt and pepper. Stir in the olive oil, and taste for salt and pepper.

Makes about 2 cups.

Spicy Meatballs Braised with Beer and Onions

We've all been to neighborhood parties where the featured dish is some kind of mystery meatball in a bland sauce. You poke in your toothpick with one hand, reach for a beer with the other, and hope for the best. But with a freezer full of delicious chicken and turkey sausages you can amaze your friends and neighbors with a fantastic array of flavorful meatballs, served in a variety of tangy sauces. One of our favorite meatball dishes features our Spicy Louisiana Sausage braised in dark beer, although you could use the Mediterranean Sausage or the Southwest Green Chile Sausage in this recipe just as well. If you'd like a slightly sweeter sauce, add a tablespoon of brown sugar or molasses.

1 pound Spicy Louisiana Sausage (page 18),
    Mediterranean Sausage (page 24), or Southwest Green
    Chile Sausage (page 20)
1 cup fresh bread crumbs
1 egg
3 tablespoons olive oil

3 cups finely chopped onions
1 bottle (12 ounces) dark lager beer or dark ale
1 cup chicken or beef stock
2 tablespoons coarse-grained mustard
1 tablespoon brown sugar or molasses (optional)

In a large bowl, mix together the sausage, bread crumbs, and egg. Squeeze and knead the mixture until well blended. Shape into meatballs, using about 1 tablespoon of the mixture for appetizer-sized meatballs about 1 inch in diameter. Heat the oil over medium heat in a large skillet and lightly brown the meatballs on all sides, about 7 minutes. Remove them with a slotted spoon and set aside.

Add the onion to the same pan and sauté over medium heat for 10 minutes until lightly colored. Add the remaining ingredients and bring to a boil. Simmer uncovered for 10 minutes. Put in the meatballs and cook until the sauce just begins to thicken, about 5 minutes. If the sauce is not thick enough, continue to cook until ready.

Makes 20 to 30 meatballs, serves 6 to 8 as appetizers.

MORE MAGNIFICENT MEATBALLS

To make other delicious meatballs, use the ingredients listed in our meatloaf and stuffed vegetable recipes, and follow the preceding directions. You might want to vary the braising liquid to suit the style of cooking, using apple cider, red or white wine, dry sherry, or light lager.

Kids' Favorite Chicken and Apple Meat Loaf with Cider Gravy (page 175)
Sicilian Meat Loaf (page 178)
More Meat Loaf Variations (page 179)
Tomatoes Stuffed with Italian Sausage (page 182)
Creole Stuffed Squash (page 183)
Mediterranean Stuffed Peppers (page 184)

Stuffed Sausage Bread

This is one of the most versatile and delicious recipes in this book. In fact, it is more a technique than a recipe. You can follow our directions for this savory stuffed bread, which makes a wonderful appetizer or light lunch, or you can introduce your own variations for both the stuffing and the dough. We suggest using one of the excellent frozen bread doughs available these days, but you can, of course, use your own favorite dough recipe with our stuffing or one of your own devising. Following this recipe we have listed some of our own suggestions for variations. Use your imagination and enjoy!

1 tablespoon olive oil, plus a little more for baking sheet
½ pound Italian Turkey and Sun-Dried Tomato Sausage (page 22), Southwest Green Chile Sausage (page 20), or Chicken and Apple Sausage (page 16)
1 cup chopped onion
½ cup chopped cooked potato

¾ cup freshly shredded mozzarella cheese
¼ cup freshly grated Parmesan cheese
½ cup chopped green olives
½ cup chopped green onions, green and white parts
1 package frozen white bread dough or your favorite recipe
1 egg beaten with 1 tablespoon water

In a large skillet, heat the oil over medium-high heat. Brown the sausage for 5 minutes, stirring and breaking it up as it cooks. Put in the chopped onion and cook 5 minutes more. Add the potato and cook for 1 more minute. In a large bowl, combine the sausage mixture with both cheeses, the olives, and green onions. Cool the filling while you prepare the dough. Follow the package instructions up to rolling out the frozen bread dough or use your own recipe. Preheat the oven to 350°F.

Divide the dough in half, and roll each piece into a 10 x 12-inch rectangle. Brush the edges with egg wash and spread half the filling to within ½ inch of the edges. Roll up the dough jelly-roll style and brush the seams and edges with egg wash, pinching to make a seal. Repeat with the other half of the dough and filling. Place on an oiled baking sheet and bake until lightly browned, about 25 minutes. (It is all right if a little filling seeps out during baking.) Let cool, slice, and serve warm.

Makes 20 to 25 slices, serves 4 to 6 as an appetizer.

Here are some suggestions: Vary the sausage and tie in other ingredients with the main flavorings, for instance, Mediterranean Sausage (page 24) with black olives and garlic or Chinese Black Mushroom Sausage (page 26) with chopped black beans and ginger. Instead of potato, try cooked broccoli, chard, or spinach; use Swiss or Cheddar cheese in place of mozzarella and Parmesan; substitute chopped sun-dried tomatoes, fire-roasted chiles (page 20) or pickled peppers for the olives. Other doughs that are delicious include egg bread, potato bread, brioche, beer bread, or pizza dough.

You may also change the size and shape of the loaf itself, making small individual loaves instead of one large one for slicing. And you can put all the filling into the center of the loaf (this works especially well for individual loaves), rather than rolling it up jelly-roll style. To do this, simply place ½ cup filling in the center of a 6-inch circle of rolled-out dough. Fold up the sides to form a rectangular, dinner-sized roll, and bake in a preheated 350°F oven until done, 25 to 30 minutes. These rolls make great substitutes for sandwiches for lunch and are wonderful with a salad for a light summer dinner.

Spicy Louisiana Sausage Skewers with Red Pepper Coulis

o make these delicious and colorful appetizers you can form balls of our Spicy Louisiana Sausage around wooden skewers or stuff the sausage into casings (see To Make Link Sausages, page 15), and then cut the links into chunks. Other master sausage recipes that could be used in this recipe are our Southwest Green Chile Sausage (page 20) and Italian Turkey and Sun-Dried Tomato Sausage (page 22).

---

8 to 10 wooden skewers
$^{1}/_{2}$ pound Spicy Louisiana Sausage (page 18), formed into 1-inch balls, or stuffed into casings and cut into 1-inch rounds

2 medium-sized red onions, cut into 1-inch chunks
2 green bell peppers, seeded, deveined, and cut into 1-inch chunks
Red Pepper Coulis (following)

Preheat the broiler or prepare coals for grilling. On 8 to 10 skewers, arrange a 2- to 3-inch row of sausage balls between chunks of onions and peppers. Or alternate 1-inch pieces of links with the onions and peppers. Grill over medium-hot coals or under the broiler for 4 to 5 minutes per side or until sausage is firm and cooked. Serve with generous dollops of coulis.

Serves 4 as an appetizer.

Red Pepper Coulis

....

This bright and flavorful sauce is not only a wonderful accompaniment to these skewers, but is also delicious on grilled fish, chicken breasts, and pork or lamb chops. Freeze any leftover coulis and use it for last-minute meals.

2 tablespoons olive oil
2 cloves garlic, minced
1 yellow onion, chopped
2 red bell peppers, seeded, deveined, and chopped
1/4 cup sun-dried tomatoes packed in olive oil,* chopped

1 tablespoon balsamic or red wine vinegar
1/4 cup chopped fresh basil
Yogurt, cream, or water for diluting sauce

* See Glossary

Heat the olive oil in a heavy skillet. Add the garlic, onion, red peppers, and sun-dried tomatoes. Cover and cook over medium heat for about 10 minutes, stirring and shaking the pan occasionally, until the peppers are soft. Add the vinegar and basil. Purée the mixture in a blender or food processor; add yogurt, cream, or water to dilute to the desired consistency of thick cream.

Makes about 1 1/2 cups coulis.

Lalime's Southwest Green Chile Burrito

Lalime's is a great neighborhood restaurant situated in one of the best neighborhoods for food in the entire San Francisco Bay Area. Located just down from Berkeley's Gourmet Gulch, the restaurant has as its neighbors some of the area's finest purveyors of produce, poultry, and seafood. And just down the street are wonderful bakeries, delicatessens, and even a world-class nursery, if you want to pick up a few exotic kitchen herbs. In a neighborhood like this, you really have to be spectacular to shine. And chef/owner Haig Krikorian and executive chef Frances Wilson turn out dramatic, fresh-tasting food that is both light and exciting. This recipe is adapted from one of their most popular menu items. You can slice the burritos into rounds to serve as an appetizer as we suggest, or leave them whole for a first course or for a main course accompanied with our Southwest Green Chile Sausage and Cabbage Salad (page 115).

1 tablespoon olive oil
1 pound Southwest Green Chile Sausage (page 20)
1 cup sliced fresh mushrooms
1/2 red onion, sliced
1 small zucchini, sliced
1 small yellow crookneck squash, sliced
2 cups cooked black beans (page 196)
1 3/4 cups grated sharp Cheddar cheese
1 teaspoon finely chopped garlic

1 teaspoon ground cumin
1/2 teaspoon puréed chipotle chiles (page 212)
8 flour tortillas (9-inch)

Accompaniments
Chipotle Sour Cream (page 212)
Haig's Cilantro Pesto (page 215)
Salsa Cruda (page 213)

Heat the olive oil in a large skillet over medium-high heat, and fry the sausage for 3 minutes, breaking it apart as it cooks. Add the mushrooms, onion, zucchini, and yellow squash, and sauté over medium heat until vegetables are tender, about 5 more minutes, stirring often. Transfer to a large bowl and mix in beans, cheese, garlic, cumin, and chipotle purée.

Preheat the oven to 400°F. Place ½ to ¾ cup of the filling in the center of the browned side of each tortilla and fold sides and ends together to make a burrito. Put the filled burritos on a lightly oiled baking sheet, brush the tops lightly with oil, and bake until lightly browned, about 5 to 7 minutes. Slice into rounds if serving as an appetizer. Serve with bowls of Chipotle Sour Cream, Haig's Cilantro Pesto, and Salsa Cruda.

Serves 16 as an appetizer or party snack, 8 as a main course.

Beer and Sausage Tasting Party with Breads and Condiments

With a freezer stocked with our sausage blends, you have the basis for a party that is simple to set up and can be a lot of fun for you and your friends. The idea is to taste the various sausages with an assortment of condiments and breads and then to match these delicious snacks with an array of flavorful beers. Depending on how you want to set it up, your party can feature light hors d'oeuvre or can turn into a full meal, especially if you add a lentil salad (see Marlene's Mediterranean Lentil Salad, page 120) or pasta salad (see Spaghettini and Crispy Sausage Salad, page 118, and Mediterranean Orzo Salad, page 119).

We suggest you start out with an hors d'oeuvre party featuring three or four varieties of sausage, four or five condiments, and three or four kinds of breads (see following chart). All you have to do is set out platters with fried patties of each type of sausage and identify them with tags placed on toothpicks. Put the condiments into separate bowls and set out baskets of sliced bread. Serve with an assortment of three or four different types of beers—lager, pale ale, dark ale, and stout, for example. Let your guests dig in, mix, match, and compare the various sausage, condiment, bread, and beer combinations. Then they can spend the rest of the evening arguing about which they liked best, going back to sample their favorites, trying new combinations. This makes for animated conversation and a lively party, to say the least.

Following is a chart of our recommendations of condiments, breads, and beers to go with each sausage. For each sausage type, pick two or three condiments and two or three breads, along with a couple of different beers. But these are just suggestions. You and your friends should do your own experiments to see what combinations you most enjoy. The possbilities, if you think about it, are infinite—which could keep you happily busy tasting and talking for quite some time.

SAUSAGE	CONDIMENT	BREAD	BEER
Chicken and Apple	*Nancy's Corn Relish	Potato	Shell's Pilsner
	Honey Mustard	Biscuits	Anchor Steam
	*Sautéed Apple Slices	*Waffles	Anchor Porter
	*Green Tomato & Red Pepper Relish	*Corn Cakes	Pete's Ale
Spicy Louisiana	*Lime Pickled Onions	French Rolls	Sierra Nevada Pale Ale
	*Creole Mustard Sauce	*Corn Cakes	Dixie Beer
	*Roasted Eggplant and Fresh Tomato Vinaigrette	Focaccia	Dock Street Amber Ale
	*Red Pepper Coulis	Soft Rolls	Samuel Adams Lager
Italian Turkey and Sun-Dried Tomato	*Fresh Tomato Vinaigrette	Focaccia	Rainier Ale
	*Fresh Tomato & Basil Sauce	*Waffles	Red Tail Ale
	*Greek Caper Sauce	Pita Rounds	Schell Wheat
	*Red Pepper Coulis	*Crostini	Boulder Amber Ale
Mediterranean	*Cucumber & Yogurt Sauce	Pita Rounds	Grant's Celtic Ale
	*Haig's Cilantro Pesto	Sesame Crackers	Widmer Weizen Beer
	*Green Tomato & Red Pepper Relish	Lavosh	Ballantine Ale
	*Lime Pickled Onions	Flour Tortillas	Corona
Thai Chicken and Turkey	*Nancy's Asian Dipping Sauce	Flour Tortillas	Tsing-Tao
	*Mango Vinaigrette	Sesame Buns	Sapporo
	*Haig's Cilantro Pesto	Rice Wrappers	Singha
	*Korean Dipping Sauce	*Corn Cakes	Kirin
Chinese Black Mushroom	*Hoisin Onions	Sesame Buns	Oktoberfest
	*Ginger Orange Dressing	Lavosh	Grant's Scottish Ale
	*Mango Vinaigrette	Flour Tortillas	Pilsner Urquell
	*Haig's Cilantro Pesto	*Corn Cakes	Guinness Stout
Southwest Green Chile	*Salsa Cruda	*Corn Cakes	Bohemia
	*Guacamole	Corn Tortillas	Carta Blanca
	*Chipolte Sour Cream Sauce	Cornbread	Dos Equis
	*Lime Pickled Onions	Bolillos	Red Stripe

*indicates recipes in the book—see index.

Mediterranean Sausage and Spinach Turnovers

Phyllo, paper-thin dough (also called filo) used in Turkish and Greek cooking, makes turning out light and flaky pastry a breeze. The dough is sold prerolled in the freezer department of most supermarkets and must be thawed overnight in the refrigerator before using. If you're the plan-ahead type, you can make up these little pastry hors d'oeuvre, freeze them on cookie sheets, and pack them away in freezer bags. When you are ready to use them, simply place the frozen turnovers on a cookie sheet and bake as directed below, adding an extra 5 minutes to compensate for the frozen centers. In the following recipe, and in handling phyllo in general, it's best to purchase a pastry brush. It makes the job a whole lot easier. Also take care that the phyllo is covered with damp towel when you are not working with it.

Salt as needed
1 bunch (12 ounces) spinach, well washed
1/2 pound Mediterranean Sausage (page 24), Southwest
    Green Chile Sausage (page 20), or Spicy Louisiana

Sausage (page 18)
1 to 2 sticks (1/4 to 1/2 pound) unsalted butter, melted, or 1/2
    to 1 cup olive oil
10 sheets phyllo pastry, thawed overnight in the refrigerator

---

Bring a 3- to 4-quart pot of lightly salted water to a boil. Add the spinach and blanch for 30 seconds. Drain and cool the spinach under cold running water. Drain again and squeeze out as much moisture as you can. Finely chop the spinach, and mix it together with the sausage meat in a bowl.

Brush 2 baking sheets with melted butter or olive oil. (For flavor we prefer butter, which also provides for better browning of the pastry. If you plan to freeze the turnovers, do not grease the baking sheets.) Place a single sheet of phyllo on your working surface, keeping the rest covered with a lightly damp towel to prevent the sheets of dough from drying out. Brush the sheet with melted butter or oil, and cover the first sheet with another sheet of phyllo. Brush it with the melted butter or oil. Cut the double sheet of phyllo into 5 strips, each 3 to 4 inches wide. Put a heaping teaspoon of the sausage mixture about 1 inch from the bottom. Fold the right-hand corner over the filling to form a triangle. Brush lightly with the butter or oil. Continue folding the triangle up the entire length of the strip, brushing each fold with the butter or oil (exactly the same technique used to fold up the American flag). Repeat the procedure for the remaining phyllo. As you finish turnovers, place them on the cookie sheets. At this point they can be baked or securely covered with plastic wrap and frozen.

To bake, preheat the oven to 350°F. Bake the triangles until they are golden brown and flaky, 20 to 25 minutes (allow 5 minutes extra for frozen turnovers). Before serving, allow the turnovers to cool for a few minutes so your guests won't burn their tongues in the feeding frenzy that usually occurs when these tasty pastries appear.

Makes 25 turnovers.

Thai Sausage Satay

Satay originated in Indonesia and consists of small wooden skewers of marinated meats—chicken, beef, pork, or lamb. These skewers are quickly grilled and served with a spicy peanut sauce. In America, satay is a popular appetizer served in Thai, Vietnamese, and Cambodian restaurants. Instead of skewering small pieces of meat, we form our Thai Chicken and Turkey Sausage around wooden skewers and grill them. You could also stuff the sausage into casings (see To Make Sausage Links, page 15) and cut the links into 1-inch chunks. This recipe is also delicious with our Chinese Black Mushroom Sausage (page 26).

1 pound Thai Chicken and Turkey Sausage (page 28)
8 to 10 wooden skewers

Thai Peanut Sauce (following)

Form the sausage around 8 to 10 wooden skewers, molding it with your hands to make a 5- or 6-inch cigar shape on the skewer. Grill or broil, turning often, until firm and done, 7 to 10 minutes. Serve with peanut sauce.

Serves 6 to 8 as an appetizer, 4 as a dish in a multicourse Thai dinner.

Thai Peanut Sauce

This sweet and spicy sauce is great with satay made from sausage, chicken or other meats. It is also enjoyable on grilled shrimp or fish, or as a dip for shrimp chips.

1 tablespoon peanut oil
1 medium onion, finely chopped
¹/₂ cup peanut butter (crunchy or smooth)
1 cup thick coconut milk*
1 tablespoon brown sugar

1 tablespoon cayenne or 2 teaspoons Thai chili paste*
2 tablespoons dark soy sauce
Juice of 1 lime

* See Glossary

In a small saucepan, heat the peanut oil over medium heat and sauté the onion until translucent, about 5 minutes. Stir in the remaining ingredients and continue to stir until the sauce comes to a boil. Pour into a small bowl and serve with sausage skewers. Peanut sauce will keep, covered, in the refrigerator for up to a week.

Makes about 1¹/₂ cups.

Savory Thai Seafood and Sausage Dumplings

These savory dumplings are absolutely simple to make and downright irresistible. Using premade round wonton wrappers, our Chinese Black Mushroom Sausage, and chopped seafood, you can turn out these tasty dumplings quicker than a professional dim sum chef, and with just as good results. Just tuck the sausage mixed with seafood in the wrappers and steam the dumplings to perfection in a few minutes. Make up some of Nancy's Asian Dipping Sauce or Korean Dipping Sauce for a dim sum feast, with a bottle of Tsing-Tao or Sapporo beer on the side. Use the seafood of your choice, alone or in combination. Raw shrimp, rock shrimp, or scallops are all delicious as are lobster or crawfish tails. The seafood should be impeccably fresh and peeled and deveined, if necessary.

1 cup coarsely chopped seafood (see above)
2 cups (about 1/2 pound) Chinese Black Mushroom Sausage
    (page 26), Thai Chicken and Turkey Sausage (page 28),
    or other spicy fresh sausage

20 to 25 round wonton wrappers*
Nancy's Asian Dipping Sauce (following) or Korean
    Dipping Sauce (page 51)
* See Glossary

In a large bowl, mix together the seafood and sausage. To make the dumplings, press a wonton wrapper into the curved palm of your hand. Scoop about 1 tablespoon of the filling into the small cup made in the center of the wrapper. Using the fingers of both hands, gently gather and fold the sides of the wrapper to make natural pleats. Squeeze the top and sides of the wrapper together to make sure it forms around the filling. Tap the dumpling on a flat surface so that it can stand upright. Repeat until all wrappers and stuffing are used. Place in a Chinese steamer or on an oiled plate over boiling water in a covered pot (see page 53), and steam until the filling is firm, 15 to 20 minutes. Serve at once with one or both of the dipping sauces.

Makes 20 to 25 dumplings, serves 6 as an appetizer.

Nancy's Asian Dipping Sauce

....

BRUCE SAYS:

"I FIRST TASTED THIS DELICIOUS AND EASY-TO-PREPARE SAUCE AT MY WIFE NANCY OAKES'S RESTAURANT, BOULEVARD, IN SAN FRANCISCO. IT'S A FANTASTIC DIPPING SAUCE FOR SEAFOOD, AND CAN ALSO BE USED AS A QUICK DRESSING FOR A THAI SALAD."

Try this tangy sauce with Savory Thai Seafood and Sausage Dumplings (page 47), Tiger Prawns Stuffed with Asian Sausage (page 49) or Pot Stickers Filled with Chinese Black Mushroom Sausage (page 52).

---

2 cups Sriracha Thai sweet chili sauce*
1 cup rice vinegar*
1/2 cup Southeast Asian fish sauce* or soy sauce
Juice of 2 limes

3 tablespoons finely chopped fresh ginger
1/4 cup finely chopped green onions, white and green parts
Asian hot chili oil* to taste (optional)
* See Glossary

Mix together the ingredients in a bowl and serve. The sauce will keep covered in the refrigerator for 7 to 10 days.

Makes 3 1/2 to 4 cups.

Tiger Prawns Stuffed with Asian Sausage

We used Asian tiger prawns for this unusual and mouthwatering appetizer, but any large shrimp or even small lobster tails would do as well. The trick is to stuff the curve of the shrimp's belly with a spicy sausage, and bake them in a hot oven. We used our Thai Chicken and Turkey Sausage, but our Chinese Black Mushroom Sausage or another flavorful fresh sausage would also be delicious. Let your guests dip the prawns into Nancy's Asian Dipping Sauce or a commercial Thai sauce such as Sriracha chilli sauce (see Glossary).

16 large raw shrimp (about ³/₄ pound total), peeled
and deveined
¹/₂ pound Thai Chicken and Turkey Sausage (page 28) or
Chinese Black Mushroom Sausage (page 26)

Peanut oil as needed to oil baking pan
Nancy's Asian Dipping Sauce (page 48) or other
dipping sauce

Preheat the oven to 450°F. Place the shrimp on an oiled baking sheet so that they form semicircular "C" shapes. Place about 1 tablespoon of the sausage within the semicircle of each shrimp. Pack the sausage tightly and make sure the filling is even with the sides of the shrimp. You can secure the tips of the shrimp with *wooden* toothpicks, if you like, but there is really no need. When the shrimp cook, they will tighten up to secure the filling.

Bake until the shrimp are pink and the sausage meat is firm, about 10 minutes. Serve at once with dipping sauce.

Serves 4 as an appetizer.

Korean Green Onion and Sausage Cakes

These spicy cakes make a great appetizer, lunch, or light dinner and are equally delicious hot or at room temperature. Traditionally the ingredients in the pancakes are bound together by a paste of ground mung beans and rice. We've substituted flour, which gives a slightly different texture, but makes a perfectly acceptable alternative. You can use many other fillings in these versatile and easy-to-make cakes: Diced shrimp, zucchini, scallops, oysters, lobster, yellow onion, bell pepper, or chiles all work well, separately or combined. Let your refrigerator and your imagination be your guide. Although one cake makes an ample serving for lunch or a light dinner, you have two options if you want to serve the cakes as an appetizer or first course. You can cut a large cake into six to eight wedges or you can make individual two- to three-inch cakes.

½ tablespoon vegetable oil
1 pound Chinese Black Mushroom Sausage (page 26) or
*   Thai Chicken and Turkey Sausage (page 28)*
1½ cups all-purpose flour
6 eggs, lightly beaten
8 green onions, white and green parts, finely chopped
1 medium carrot, shredded
Peanut oil as needed

2 teaspoons Asian sesame oil*
½ teaspoon salt
1 cup water or more if needed
1 cup bean sprouts
1 red bell pepper, seeded, deveined, and cut into fine
*   julienne strips about 2 inches long*

* See Glossary

Heat the vegetable oil in a skillet over medium-high heat, and fry the sausage for 5 minutes, breaking it up as it cooks. Remove the sausage from the pan and reserve.

To make the batter, beat the flour into the eggs in a large bowl. Add the green onions, carrot, 1 tablespoon peanut oil, sesame oil, and salt. Beat in the water to make a smooth, medium-thick batter. Add more water if necessary. Let the batter stand for 20 to 30 minutes.

Heat 2 teaspoons peanut oil in a 9-inch nonstick skillet over medium-high heat. To make large cakes, pour in ¼ of the batter (about ⅔ cup). Sprinkle the surface of the pancake with ¼ each of the sausage, bean sprouts, and red bell pepper. Cook the pancake 3 to 4 minutes, until the edges begin to curl and the bottom is light brown. Turn or flip the pancake, and cook until the pancake is cooked through and nicely browned, 2 to 3 minutes. Transfer the pancake to a warm serving platter and repeat the process to make a total of 4 large cakes. Leave cakes whole for single servings or cut each cake into 6 wedges for appetizers. To make minicakes, follow the same procedures, but make four 2- to 3-inch pancakes at a time.

Serves 8 to 10 as an appetizer, 4 as a first course or a dish in a multicourse Asian dinner.

Korean Dipping Sauce

....

This tart, nutty sauce is a spicy accompaniment to our Korean Green Onion and Sausage Cakes (page 50), but it is also delicious as a dipping sauce for Tiger Prawns Stuffed with Asian Sausage (page 49), Pot Stickers Filled with Chinese Black Mushroom Sausage (page 52), or Thai Sausage Satay (page 45). It also makes a great sauce for grilled shrimp, scallops, bell peppers, or mushrooms, skewered separately or in any combination.

2 teaspoons toasted sesame seeds (following)
1/4 cup chopped fresh cilantro (optional)
1 tablespoon grated fresh ginger
1/4 cup soy sauce
2 tablespoons rice vinegar or cider vinegar

1/4 cup finely chopped green onions, white and green parts
2 teaspoons Asian sesame oil*
2 teaspoons sugar

* See Glossary

Put all the ingredients into a jar and shake to mix thoroughly or mix well in a bowl. This versatile dipping sauce will keep in the refrigerator in a sealed jar for 1 week.

Makes about 3/4 cup.

TO TOAST SESAME SEEDS

Put 1/2 cup sesame seeds into a small heavy skillet over medium heat. Sprinkle lightly with salt, and continuously shake the pan until the seeds are lightly brown and give off a toasty aroma. Immediately transfer the seeds to a plate or bowl. Cool and store in a closed jar at room temperature for up to 1 month.

Pot Stickers filled with Chinese Black Mushroom Sausage

In the 1960s and '70s northern-style Chinese restaurants became the vogue, replacing the Cantonese restaurants most of us were used to. One of the most popular dishes that diners (and especially kids) discovered were pot stickers—fried or steamed dumplings of pasta dough filled with savory pork and spices. Most of the time, pot stickers are lightly browned on the bottom and then steamed—a technique that requires an intricate fold that we have yet to master. Our version uses wonton wrappers folded into half moons and then browned on both sides. These wrappers are thinner than the usual pot sticker dough and, when stuffed with one of our Asian sausages, the results are light and delicious. These zesty dumplings are simple to make. We use our Chinese Black Mushroom Sausage, but our Thai Chicken and Turkey Sausage (page 28) is equally good. And, surprisingly, our Chicken and Apple Sausage (page 16) also works well. Serve the pot stickers with little bottles or bowls of soy sauce and other Asian condiments and let diners make their own dipping sauce.

Or use Nancy's Asian Dipping Sauce (page 48) or our Korean Dipping Sauce (page 51).

1/2 pound Chinese Black Mushroom Sausage (page 26)
2 cups finely shredded napa cabbage or green cabbage
1/4 cup finely chopped green onions, white and green parts
1/2 cup chopped fresh cilantro (optional)
1 tablespoon Chinese brown bean paste* (optional)
Salt and freshly ground black pepper to taste

25 to 30 round wonton wrappers*
Peanut oil for frying
Soy sauce, rice vinegar,* Asian hot chili oil,* and Asian sesame oil* for dipping sauce

* See Glossary

In a large bowl, mix together the sausage, cabbage, green onions, and, if using, the cilantro and brown bean paste. Make a small patty, fry, and taste for salt and pepper. Place a tablespoon or more of the filling in the center of each wonton wrapper, fold in half, brush edges with water and seal by pressing together. (At this point, the pot stickers can be spread on a cookie sheet, frozen, and packed into freezer bags for future use.)

To cook, coat the bottom of a heavy 12-inch, nonstick skillet with peanut oil and heat over medium heat. Panfry 8 to 10 pot stickers at a time until golden brown, 5 to 6 minutes (frozen pot stickers will take about a minute longer). Turn pot stickers over, and brown the other side for 3 to 4 minutes more. Drain on paper towels and serve at once with fixings for dipping sauce.

Makes 25 to 30 dumplings, serves 6.

Chinese Stuffed Mushrooms

Simple to prepare, these delicious mushrooms are stuffed with sausage and then steamed. In classic Chinese cooking, they would be served, covered with sauce, as part of a dim sum lunch. We prefer to offer them as appetizers without the sauce. If you like, accompany them with Nancy's Asian Dipping Sauce (page 48) or our Korean Dipping Sauce (page 51).

20 to 25 large Chinese dried black mushrooms*
or Japanese dried shiitake mushrooms*
¹/₂ pound Chinese Black Mushroom Sausage (page 26)

Soy sauce to taste

* See Glossary

Place the mushrooms in a heatproof bowl and cover them completely with boiling water. Soak them for at least 30 minutes or as long as 2 to 3 hours. Remove mushrooms, and cut off and discard tough stems. Mound about a tablespoon of the sausage in the gill side of each mushroom. Sprinkle with soy sauce and place them, stuffing side up, on a steam basket or heatproof plate. Repeat until all the mushrooms are stuffed.

Steam the mushrooms in a Chinese steamer or makeshift steamer (following) over boiling water for 20 minutes. Serve the mushrooms with or without the dipping sauces mentioned above.

Makes 20 to 25, serves 6.

A MAKESHIFT CHINESE STEAMER

If you don't have a Chinese steamer, you'll need to set up a makeshift steamer. Place 2 inches of water in a pot larger than the plate the food is on. Put in a couple of empty tuna cans, small heatproof cups, or whatever else will safely support the plate just above the water. Cover the pot tightly with a lid or foil, bring the water to a boil, and steam the food until done.

Sandwiches

It's hard to think of sandwiches without sausage. Sausages of every type imaginable are found on some of the world's greatest sandwiches from the Italian hero to the Louisiana po'boy. In our recipes we've adapted our poultry-based, low-fat sausages to some of the classic sandwiches, such as our Italian Super Hero (page 56), Louisiana Po'Boy with Creole Mustard Sauce (page 60), Chicken and Apple Sausage Club Sandwich (page 58), and Mexican Torta with Lime Pickled Onions (page 59).

We've also come up with a few original combinations that extend the concept of the sandwich a bit. Our Thai Sausage Roll with Mango Vinaigrette (page 55) and Chinese Sausage Sandwich with Hoisin Onions (page 61) are unusual and delicious Asian variations on the sandwich theme.

Thai Sausage Roll with Mango Vinaigrette

Street food in Bangkok is some of the best in the world. Sidewalks are crowded with vendors offering grilled meats and fish, spicy salads, sandwiches, snacks, soups—all bursting with the bright and lively flavors that make Thai cooking so appealing. Our Thai Chicken and Turkey Sausage has plenty of those flavors—chiles, lemongrass, garlic, basil, cilantro. In this tasty sandwich, we wrap the zesty sausage in a flour tortilla and add our gingery Mango Vinaigrette to wake up the taste buds. Wash it all down with a cold Singha beer.

For Each Sandwich
¼ pound Thai Chicken and Turkey Sausage (page 28), formed into an oblong patty
1 flour tortilla

1 to 2 tablespoons Mango Vinaigrette (page 219)
1 or 2 green onions, white and green parts, thinly sliced lengthwise
Cilantro sprigs (optional)

Preheat the oven to 300°F. Panfry or grill the sausage patty over medium-high heat for 3 to 5 minutes on each side until browned and cooked through. Set aside and keep warm.

Wrap the tortilla in aluminum foil and warm in the oven for 10 minutes. Place the sausage patty in the tortilla, top with a tablespoon or two of Mango Vinaigrette, some green onions, and sprigs of cilantro, if using. Roll up and serve.

Makes 1 sandwich.

Italian Super Hero

....

DENIS SAYS:

"STANDING ON THE SIDEWALK IN NEW YORK'S LITTLE ITALY AND BITING DOWN ON MY FIRST HERO SANDWICH IS ONE OF MY EARLIEST FOOD MEMORIES. THE COMBINATION OF SPICY GRILLED SAUSAGE, ROASTED GREEN PEPPERS, AND FRIED ONIONS ON A CRUSTY ITALIAN ROLL WAS A JOYFUL SURPRISE TO MY IRISH TASTEBUDS. WOW! I THOUGHT, JUICE RUNNING DOWN MY CHIN AND ONTO MY SHIRT, THIS SURE BEATS MASHED POTATOES AND GRAVY. AND WHO CARES ABOUT GREASY FINGERS OR STAINS ON THE SHIRT WHEN SOMETHING TASTES THIS GOOD?"

Another style of hero sandwich combines layers of Italian cold cuts, cheeses, sliced onions, and pickled peppers on Italian rolls drizzled with oil and vinegar. In our recipe we've borrowed elements from both of these great sandwiches to make a true Italian Super Hero.

For Each Sandwich

1/4 pound Italian Turkey and Sun-Dried Tomato Sausage (page 22), formed into an oblong patty about the size of the roll

1 Italian or French roll (5 to 6 inches), split

Roasted Eggplant and Fresh Tomato Vinaigrette (page 210)

2 thin slices provolone or fontina cheese

4 to 6 Italian pickled peppers (peperoncini) or 4 to 6 slices roasted red bell pepper (page 20)

4 thin slices raw red onion

Panfry or grill the sausage patty over medium-high heat for 3 to 5 minutes per side, until browned and cooked through. Set aside and keep warm.

Generously spread both halves of the roll with Roasted Eggplant and Tomato Vinaigrette. Place the patty on the bottom half. Cover with the sliced cheese, peppers, and onions. Squeeze the 2 halves of the roll together, and eat while the sausage is still quite warm and the cheese slightly softened.

Makes 1 sandwich.

Pita with Mediterranean Sausage and Greek Caper Sauce

Street food is one of our passions. Some of the spiciest and tastiest food imaginable is found on the crowded streets of the great cities: New Orleans, Naples, Bangkok, Hong Kong to name a few. And in New York, Chicago, and Athens—any place with a substantial Greek population—you're likely to find street vendors hawking spicy sausages or bits of roast lamb tucked into pita bread with tart and flavorful sauces. The sauces are the key to these delicious snacks. They are often family secrets handed down from generation to generation and usually include favorite Mediterranean flavors like garlic, lemon, capers, and olive oil. Our Greek Caper Sauce isn't a secret any more, but it is very tasty in sandwiches or on grilled fish or chicken. We pair it here with our Mediterranean Sausage and our refreshing Cucumber and Yogurt Sauce for a piquant and satisfying sandwich. Serve it with Greek pickled banana peppers and a Greek salad of onions, tomatoes, olives, and crumbled feta cheese for a substantial lunch or light dinner.

For Each Sandwich
¼ pound Mediterranean Sausage (page 24), formed into an oblong patty
1 pita round

Greek Caper Sauce (page 217)
Cucumber and Yogurt Sauce (page 216)
¼ cup coarsely chopped ripe tomatoes
2 tablespoons coarsely chopped fresh cilantro (optional)

Preheat the oven to 300°F. Panfry or grill the sausage patty over medium-high heat for 3 to 5 minutes on a side until browned and cooked through. Set aside and keep warm.

Wrap the pita bread in aluminum foil and warm in the oven for 10 minutes. Cut the top off the pita and open up the round to form a pocket. Fill the pocket first with the sausage patty and then drizzle with the Greek Caper Sauce. Spoon in a couple of tablespoons of the Cucumber and Yogurt Sauce, the chopped tomatoes, and cilantro, if using.

Makes 1 sandwich.

Chicken and Apple Sausage Club Sandwich

Club sandwiches are usually triple-deckers of toasted white bread layered with chicken or turkey, tomatoes, mayonnaise, and bacon. We've made our club sandwich only one layer, so it's easier to eat, and we use lean Canadian bacon instead of the fattier American version. Our Chicken and Apple Sausage provides a sweet and succulent counterpoint to the lightly smoked bacon, crisp lettuce, and ripe tomato. We suggest you use toasted home-style white bread or sliced sourdough for this hearty sandwich. Serve it with a generous scoop of Nancy's Corn Relish (page 208) and a stein of full-bodied American lager such as Samuel Adams or August Schell for the perfect summer lunch or dinner.

For Each Sandwich
¼ pound Chicken and Apple Sausage (page 16), formed into a patty about the size and shape of the bread slices
2 thin slices Canadian bacon

2 slices home-style white or sourdough bread
Mayonnaise
2 slices ripe beefsteak tomato
1 leaf iceberg lettuce

Panfry or grill the sausage patty over medium-high heat for 3 to 5 minutes per side, until browned and cooked through. Set aside and keep warm. In the same pan, fry the bacon 2 minutes on each side and reserve.

Toast the bread slices and spread each slice generously with mayonnaise. Put the sausage patty, bacon, tomato, and lettuce on 1 toast slice and cover with the other. Cut the sandwich in half and serve.

Makes 1 sandwich.

Mexican Torta with Lime Pickled Onions

Tortas are Mexican sandwiches served on soft chewy rolls called *bolillos*, filled with chicken, *carnitas* (small bits of roast pork), beef, or cheese. The sandwich is then dressed with lots of condiments: mayonnaise, guacamole, salsa, onions, etc. If you don't live near a Mexican bakery, fresh French or Italian sandwich rolls will do just fine. Serve with Lalime's Black Beans (page 196) or corn chips.

For Each Sandwich
1/4 pound Southwest Green Chile Sausage (page 20),
   formed into an oblong patty about the size of the roll
1 bolillo *or other roll, split*
Mayonnaise

1/4 cup Guacamole (page 211)
2 tablespoons or more Lime Pickled Onions (page 214)
1 tablespoon or more Salsa Cruda (page 213)
1/2 cup shredded lettuce

Panfry or grill the sausage patty over medium-high heat for 3 to 5 minutes on each side, until browned and cooked through. Set aside and keep warm.

   Spread each half of the roll with mayonnaise, place the patty on the bottom half and cover with a layer of Guacamole, some Lime Pickled Onions, and a spoonful of Salsa Cruda. Put a layer of shredded lettuce on the other half, and squeeze the halves together gently. Cut in half and serve.

Makes 1 sandwich.

Louisiana Po'Boy with Creole Mustard Sauce

....

BRUCE SAYS:

"THIS IS THE CLASSIC SALOON SANDWICH OF NEW ORLEANS. YOU BELLY UP TO THE BAR ON
A HOT SUMMER NIGHT IN SOME JOINT IN THE FRENCH QUARTER WITH THE
BAND WARMING UP IN THE CORNER, MUNCH DOWN A PO'BOY OR TWO, SIP A DIXIE BEER,
AND CONTEMPLATE THE EVENING'S COMING ADVENTURES."

Our version uses a fried or grilled patty of our Spicy Louisiana Sausage, but you could also use *chaurice, boudin,* andouille, or any hot Louisiana-style sausage.

For Each Sandwich
¼ pound Spicy Louisiana Sausage (page 18), formed into
   an oblong patty about the size of the roll
1 Italian or French roll (5 to 6 inches)
2 tablespoons or more Creole Mustard Sauce (page 207)

½ cup shredded cabbage
¼ cup thinly sliced onions
1 to 2 tablespoons mayonnaise
Dash Tabasco

Panfry or grill the sausage patty over medium-high heat for 3 to 5 minutes per side, until browned and cooked through. Set aside and keep warm.

Generously spread both halves of the roll with Creole Mustard Sauce. Toss the shredded cabbage and thinly sliced onions together with the mayonnaise and a dash of Tabasco.

Place the sausage patty on the bottom half of the roll and top with the cabbage and onion mixture. Squeeze the two halves together and bite down.

Makes 1 sandwich.

Chinese Sausage Sandwich with Hoisin Onions

Everyone who enjoys those wonderful Chinese snacks, dim sum, has certainly eaten a pork bow—a small bready bun filled with sweet Chinese barbecued pork and hoisin sauce. Usually the bun is steamed and pale white, but our favorites are sprinkled with sesame seeds and baked to a light golden brown. This sandwich recipe is inspired by these savory buns. Make sure to prepare plenty of Ginger Orange Slaw, as this crunchy, sweet and sour cabbage is absolutely delicious with the savory sandwich. Serve with cool bottles of Asian beer such as Sapporo from Japan, Tsing-Tao from China, or Singha from Thailand.

For Each Sandwich
1/4 pound Chinese Black Mushroom Sausage (page 26), formed into a round patty about the size of the bun
1 high quality sesame seed hamburger bun, split

1/2 cup Ginger Orange Slaw (following)
2 tablespoons or more Hoisin Onions (page 218)
Mayonnaise (optional)

Panfry or grill the sausage patty over medium-high heat for 3 to 5 minutes per side, until browned and cooked through. Set aside and keep warm.

Lightly toast the split hamburger bun. Place the sausage patty on the bottom half of the bun, and cover with Ginger Orange Slaw, and then the Hoisin Onions. If you like, you may spread the top half of the bun with mayonnaise before you place it on top of the sandwich. Serve at once with additional Ginger Orange Slaw on the side.

Makes 1 sandwich.

Ginger Orange Slaw

This easy-to-make gingery slaw is delicious as a condiment on sandwiches, and also makes a wonderful side dish with Asian seafood or fish like our Tiger Prawns Stuffed with Asian Sausage (page 49) or Edy's Chinese Stuffed Fish (page 152).

4 cups shredded napa cabbage or green cabbage
½ cup or more Ginger Orange Dressing (page 126)

Salt and freshly ground black pepper to taste

In a salad bowl, toss the cabbage with the Ginger Orange Dressing. Taste for salt and pepper.

Serves 4.

Breakfast All Day

Breakfast All Day

Breakfast and sausage—the two words seem to go together. Our Chicken and Apple Sausage is a lighter version of the classic American breakfast sausage. You can substitute this aromatic and slightly sweet sausage wherever you would use a sage and pepper flavored patty or link. We've adapted some traditional American breakfast favorites using our Chicken and Apple Sausage *in* or *on*—not alongside—French toast (page 84), pancakes (page 74), and waffles (page 88).

But breakfast sausage doesn't have to be limited to the old standby. Some of our spiciest poultry-based sausages can be used to create original and mouth-awakening breakfasts. Our Southwest Green Chile Sausage and Potato Hash (page 65) with fried eggs or our Green Chile Sausage Soufflé (page 70) give breakfast a Southwestern flavor. Our Sausage and Creamy Eggs in Popovers (page 66) and Mediterranean Sausage Puffy Pancakes (page 75) provide flavorful hints of the south of France. And for a really exotic breakfast try our Asian-accented dishes: Chinese Black Mushroom Sausage Puffy Pancakes (page 76) and Thai Shrimp Salad Corn Cakes (page 81).

Many of our breakfast dishes also make delicious lunches or first courses for a dinner party such as our Tex-Mex Mini Corn Cakes (page 80), Tortilla Español en Sofrito (page 68), and Italian Sausage Waffles with Fresh Tomato and Basil Sauce (page 89).

Southwest Green Chile Sausage and Potato Hash

Traditionally hash is made with leftover corned beef or roast beef fried with potatoes and onions. Pleasant enough, but if you use a flavorful sausage in the hash, you can end up with an unusual and exciting dish. Both our Southwest Green Chile Sausage and the Mediterranean Sausage are delicious in hash. And you might want to experiment with more exotic flavors such as the Spicy Louisiana Sausage (page 18) or the Thai Chicken and Turkey Sausage (page 28). Our favorite way to prepare any hash is to cook the meat and potatoes the day before, and then form the hash into individual patties to panfry just before you serve them. This ensures that the hash is crisp on both sides and also saves preparation time just before you eat. The hash can either be served as is or with poached or fried eggs on top. To make a hearty lunch or main course, serve this hash with a scoop of Lalime's Black Beans (page 196) and a stack of warm corn tortillas.

3 to 4 tablespoons olive oil
1 pound Southwest Green Chile Sausage (page 20) or
    Mediterranean Sausage (page 24)
2 mild green chiles (such as Anaheim*) or 1 green bell
    pepper, seeded, deveined, and chopped
1 medium onion, chopped
2 tablespoons red wine vinegar

2 medium potatoes, cooked, peeled, and shredded
2 tablespoons heavy cream
Salt and freshly ground black pepper to taste
Salsa Cruda (page 213), Chipotle Sour Cream (page 212),
    or sour cream for garnish

* See Glossary

Put about 2 tablespoons of the olive oil in a large, nonstick skillet over medium heat. Add the sausage and fry for 5 minutes, breaking it up as it cooks. Put in the chiles and onions, add the vinegar to deglaze the pan, and scrape up any particles from the bottom. Continue cooking until the vinegar has been absorbed. Add the potatoes and cream. Cook until almost dry, about 5 minutes. The mixture should be just moist enough to hold together. Add salt and pepper to taste and let it cool. If you like, cover and refrigerate overnight.

Shape the hash into patties about 5 inches in diameter and about 1/2 inch thick. Heat the remaining olive oil in a nonstick skillet over medium heat. Fry the patties on both sides until lightly browned, about 5 to 6 minutes. Serve with Salsa Cruda and Chipotle Sour Cream or sour cream.

Serves 4 to 6.

Sausage and Creamy Eggs in Popovers

BRUCE SAYS:

"I WAS WITH FRIENDS IN THE DORDOGNE IN SOUTHERN FRANCE. WE ALL GATHERED IN THE EVENING ON THE PATIO AFTER A LONG DAY'S WALK IN THE WOODS HUNTING TRUFFLES, THE BLACK GOLD OF THE FRENCH COUNTRYSIDE. WE HAD BAGS AND BAGS FULL OF TRUFFLES, AND ENJOYED OUR TREASURE TROVE IN EVERY WAY IMAGINABLE. BUT THE SENSATION OF THE AFTERNOON WAS WARM BRIOCHES SPLIT IN HALF, FILLED WITH CREAMY SCRAMBLED EGGS, TRUFFLES, AND CRÈME FRAÎCHE."

We've adapted this memorable dish for a sumptuous American breakfast. We replaced the aromatic (and very expensive) truffles with another flavorful ingredient, sausage. If you are feeling flush, however, go ahead and add a chopped fresh truffle or two. But be careful if you do put truffles in this dish. They will be beautiful with our Chicken and Apple Sausage, but would most likely be overpowered by the Spicy Louisiana Sausage. And we've replaced the brioche with airy popovers (be sure to start these at least an hour ahead of serving).

Wagner's Puffy Popovers (following)
½ pound Chicken and Apple Sausage (page 16) or Spicy
  Louisiana Sausage (page 18)
½ stick (4 tablespoons) butter

8 eggs
3 ounces cream cheese, at room temperature
¼ cup chopped chives or green onions
Salt and freshly ground black pepper to taste

Prepare and bake popovers before starting the egg and sausage filling.

In a 10- to 12-inch nonstick skillet, fry the sausage over medium heat in 1 tablespoon of the butter for 4 to 5 minutes, breaking it up as it cooks. In a bowl, beat together the eggs and cream cheese. Add the remaining butter to the skillet with the sausage and melt it over medium heat. Pour in the egg and cheese mixture and, as the eggs begin to set on the bottom and sides of the pan, gently lift the cooked portion so that the uncooked egg can coat the bottom and side. Repeat, but don't stir the eggs constantly. They are done when all the eggs have thickened, but are still quite moist.

Cut off the top of each popover. Spoon out any uncooked batter remaining in the center, and fill generously with the sausage egg mixture. It's OK if some of the mixture runs over the side of the popover. Sprinkle with chives or green onions, replace the top, and serve.

Serves 6.

Wagner's Puffy Popovers

....

This popover recipe comes from Julie and Gary Wagner, who make wonderful breakfasts for the many friends who visit their Napa Valley home. Julie is a popover wizard and even has a special magic pan made of glazed pottery that produces giant airy popovers. Julie has two important tips for perfect popovers: Use only whole milk (not skim or low fat); and make sure you hand whisk the batter, as an electric mixer can overbeat the batter and it will not rise.

8 eggs
2²/₃ cups whole milk
2²/₃ cups all-purpose flour

1 teaspoon salt
1 stick (¹/₄ pound) butter, melted

Preheat the oven to 375°F. Beat the eggs in a deep bowl and beat in the milk until well blended. In another bowl, combine the flour and salt. Using a fork or pastry blender, stir the butter into the flour. Then gradually add the flour and butter mixture to the eggs, blending well with a whisk—not with an electric mixer. Thoroughly butter six ³/₄-cup custard cups or ³/₄-cup popover cups. Fill each with ¹/₂ to ²/₃ cup of batter, place them directly on the oven rack, and bake until golden, 55 minutes to 1 hour. Remove the popovers from the oven and let stand for at least 5 minutes before filling.

Makes 6 popovers.

Tortilla Español en Sofrito

If you order a "tortilla" in Spain you could be in for a surprise. Instead of the corn or flour tortilla of Mexican cuisine, you're likely to end up with a thick omelet of potatoes and onions. These savory omelets are cut into squares and served cold in tapas bars as a snack with drinks. But a more elaborate presentation might incorporate Spanish sausage and peppers in the eggs along with a piquant sauce called *sofrito*. This spicy mixture of onions, garlic, peppers, and tomatoes fried in olive oil is a mainstay in Spanish cooking and is used to flavor a wide variety of dishes from soups and stews to grilled fish, poultry, and meat. Our recipe suggests you spoon sofrito over a traditional Spanish tortilla made with flavorful sausage. We prefer our Mediterranean Sausage in this recipe, but it also works well with other spicy sausages. Serve this dish as a hearty brunch accompanied with rice with sofrito poured over it or as a tapa-style appetizer without the sauce.

Sofrito (following)
4 tablespoons olive oil
½ pound Mediterranean Sausage (page 24), Southwest Green Chile Sausage (page 20), Spicy Louisiana Sausage (page 18) or other spicy sausage (such as Spanish chorizo or hot Italian)

1 medium onion, thinly sliced
3 cups thinly sliced unpeeled red or white boiling potatoes
Salt and freshly ground black pepper to taste
8 eggs, lightly beaten
Cooked rice for accompaniment

Prepare Sofrito and keep warm while making the omelet.

Heat 2 tablespoons of the olive oil in a 10-inch nonstick skillet over medium heat and fry the sausage for 3 minutes, breaking it up as it cooks. Add the onions and continue cooking for another 3 minutes. Put in the potatoes and cook until tender, 10 to 15 minutes more, shaking the pan and turning the potatoes frequently (they don't need to be brown or crisp). Season with salt and pepper to taste.

In a large bowl combine the cooked potato mixture and the eggs. Heat the remaining 2 tablespoons oil in a clean, 10-inch nonstick skillet over medium heat. Pour in the egg and potato mixture and cook until the eggs have begun to set, about 10 minutes. Carefully invert the omelet onto a dinner plate, and slide it back into the pan with the uncooked side down. Cook until the eggs are no longer soft, 5 to 7 minutes. Transfer to a platter and let the omelet rest for 5 minutes. Cut into 6 wedges and serve covered with sofrito and accompanied with rice and more sofrito.

Serves 6.

Sofrito

....

DENIS SAYS:

"SOFRITO IS A GREAT SAUCE FOR EGGS AND CAN JUST BE SPOONED OVER A PLAIN EGG
OMELET OR FRIED EGGS. OR YOU CAN PUT SOME IN AN OVENPROOF DISH, BREAK
SOME EGGS ON TOP AND BAKE TO MAKE *HUEVOS A LA FLAMENCO,* A FAVORITE WAY TO
END A NIGHT'S CAROUSING IN THE BODEGAS AND FLAMENCO BARS OF BARCELONA'S
WILD AND WOOLY BARRIO CHINO."

2 tablespoons olive oil

¼ pound Mediterranean Sausage (page 24), Southwest
  Green Chile Sausage (page 20), or Spicy Louisiana
  Sausage (page 18)

1 medium onion, finely chopped

3 cloves garlic, chopped

1 green bell pepper, seeded, deveined, and chopped

4 ripe tomatoes, peeled, seeded, and chopped

3 tablespoons sherry (optional)

Salt and freshly ground black pepper to taste

Heat the oil in a skillet over medium heat, add the sausage, and fry for 5 minutes, breaking it up as it cooks. Put in the onion, garlic, and pepper and cook until the vegetables are soft, 5 to 7 minutes more. Add the tomatoes and sherry, if using, and cook until the mixture just begins to thicken. Taste for salt and pepper. Keep warm until ready to serve.

Makes about 2 cups.

Green Chile Sausage Soufflé

A popular dish in many Mexican restaurants is the *chile relleno*, a mild green chile stuffed with cheese, coated with a thick egg batter, and fried. In the hands of an accomplished cook, *chiles rellenos* can be light and delicious. But all too often they are made up in the morning and served later in the day. The result is heavy and greasy, often with a warmed-over taste. In addition, preparation is difficult and time consuming. A much easier but no less satisfying dish is this green chile casserole, using our Southwest Green Chile Sausage, whole green chiles, mild cheese, and eggs. It is painless to make and has far less fat and calories than the traditional fried version. An added plus is that it can be rewarmed with satisfactory results, although it also tastes pretty darned good cold. Both our Mediterranean Sausage (page 24) and Spicy Louisiana Sausage (page 18) would also work well in this dish.

Vegetable oil, for baking dish
2 cans (4 ounces each) whole, fire-roasted green chiles,*
    drained, or 8 fresh Anaheim* or poblano* chiles,
    fire-roasted and peeled (page 20)
6 ounces jack cheese, cut into ¹/₂ x 3-inch strips
¹/₂ pound Southwest Green Chile Sausage (page 20)
¹/₂ cup all-purpose flour
¹/₂ teaspoon salt

Pinch ground nutmeg
4 large eggs, separated, plus 2 egg whites
2 cups milk
Salsa Cruda (page 213) and chopped fresh cilantro
    for garnish
Warmed corn tortillas and refried beans for
    accompaniments
* See Glossary

Preheat the oven to 350°F. Oil a 9x13-inch baking dish. Cut a slit in each chile lengthwise, insert a strip of cheese into each chile, and place in the dish. Fry the sausage in a nonstick skillet over medium-high heat for 4 to 5 minutes, breaking it up as it cooks. Distribute the sausage over the top of the chiles. In a food processor or large bowl, mix the flour, salt, and nutmeg with egg yolks and milk until smooth. In a separate large bowl, beat the egg whites until they form firm peaks. Fold the yolk mixture into the whites until no white areas remain. Spoon the egg mixture over the chiles, and bake until a toothpick inserted in the center comes out clean, 12 to 15 minutes. Using a metal spatula, cut out and serve 2 chiles per person. Garnish with Salsa Cruda and chopped cilantro. Serve accompanied with corn tortillas and refried beans.

Serves 4.

IDEAS FOR LEFTOVER GREEN CHILE SAUSAGE SOUFFLÉ
....

You can cut leftovers into rectangles to use as a filling for a Mexican Torta with Lime Pickled Onions (page 59). Or reheat strips of leftover soufflé to roll into warm flour tortillas with Lalime's Black Beans (page 196) and Salsa Cruda (page 213) for a quick and delicious burrito.

Pancake Perfection from the Gurus of the Griddle

No book about sausages would be worth a weenie without talking about pancakes. Pancakes and sausage is one of those breakfast pairings like ham and eggs or doughnuts and coffee that just seem to go naturally together. And it's combinations like these that get many a slugabed stirring on cold mornings.

Full-scale breakfasts can take time to prepare, however, and some of the classics can be a bit rich for everyday eating. So these days many of us make do with a bowl of granola and fruit on weekdays and celebrate Sunday morning with an old-fashioned breakfast and *The New York Times*. Weekends give us more time to cook and enjoy traditional American breakfast favorites. And weekends allow us a little respite from counting calories and worrying about nasty lipoproteins. If you use our recipes for light, but still flavorful sausages, even the most sumptuous breakfasts need not make you worry about your waistline and cholesterol.

Northern California is blessed by two woman chefs who produce some of the best breakfasts in America and make some of the finest pancakes that ever adorned a blackened griddle. Bette Kroening of Bette's Diner in Berkeley and Margaret Fox of Cafe Beaujolais in Mendocino are the Grandes Dames of the Pancake Turner and Well Seasoned Skillet. They both provide delicious breakfasts to eager patrons at their restaurants, and they also produce packaged pancake mixes that are foolproof and delicious (see Sources, page 224). For those who want to make wonderful pancakes from scratch, these gurus of the griddle have given us the following recipes along with helpful hints on making pancakes.

Even though pancakes accompanied with patties of Chicken and Apple Sausage or Spicy Louisiana Sausage are a delicious and easy-to-make breakfast, we've gone a step further to show you how to incorporate different types of sausage into the pancake recipes themselves. This way, you can turn a tasty breakfast dish into a savory lunch, light dinner, or a scrumptious side dish. Then it's up to you to decide how to adapt and change the recipes even more to suit your own tastes and eating styles. The variations of pancakes and sausages are virtually endless—experiment and enjoy!

Bette's Puffy Pancakes

T hese huge, puffy soufflé pancakes are favorite breakfast treats at Bette's Diner in Berkeley and are the basis for our sausage-topped pancake recipes that follow. But don't start getting nervous about the word *soufflé*. Unlike traditional soufflés, these pancakes are almost foolproof (or more exactly, fall-proof). Bette's method is to start the pancakes on top of the stove and then finish them under the broiler until they are beautifully puffed and browned. Your challenge as chef and host is to make sure your guests are already seated and ready to eat at the table, so you can present them with the airy masterpieces before they begin to deflate. Watch the pancake carefully during the last couple of minutes of cooking so that you don't overcook it. An overcooked soufflé pancake will fall immediately, while a properly cooked version will stay nice and puffy all the way to the table. Then, instruct your happy diners that the proper way to eat a soufflé pancake is from the edge toward the center, because the center will continue to cook as the pancake cools.

4 egg yolks

1 cup half-and-half

1/2 cup all-purpose flour

1 1/2 tablespoons butter

2 teaspoons granulated sugar

1/2 teaspoon salt

6 egg whites

Powdered sugar and ground cinnamon for dusting

In a large bowl, beat the egg yolks with the half-and-half. Slowly add the flour, stirring just to combine. In a 10-inch nonstick skillet with an ovenproof or removable plastic handle, melt the butter. (This saves greasing the pan for pancakes later.) Stir the melted butter, sugar, and salt into the egg batter. In another large bowl, beat the egg whites until they form soft peaks and fold them into the batter.

Heat your already-greased skillet over high heat until it begins to smoke. Add 1/2 of the batter, reduce the heat to medium, and cook until the bottom is lightly browned and the batter has begun to firm up, about 5 minutes. At this point you may add any of the sausage toppings described in the following recipes.

Meanwhile, preheat the broiler. Place the skillet 4 to 5 inches away from the heat and broil until the top is browned and the center of the pancake is just set, but still soft, 4 to 5 minutes. Slide the pancake onto a serving platter, dust with powdered sugar and cinnamon, and bring it to the table pronto. Cut into 4 wedges to serve. Repeat the process for the second pancake.

Makes two 10-inch pancakes, serves 4.

Chicken and Apple Sausage Puffy Pancakes

T hese delicious pancakes are perfect for an autumn brunch or luncheon. Use tart apples such as pippins, Granny Smiths, or Winesaps.

---

2 teaspoons butter
$^1/_2$ pound Chicken and Apple Sausage (page 16), formed
    into 8 patties
1 cup peeled, cored, and sliced apple (about 1 medium apple)

$^1/_4$ teaspoon ground cinnamon
1 tablespoon sugar
1 recipe Bette's Puffy Pancakes (page 73)

Put the butter in a heavy skillet and fry the sausage patties over medium-high heat, turning once, until lightly browned on both sides, about 7 minutes total. Remove and reserve patties. Add the apples to the skillet and sprinkle with the cinnamon and sugar. Reduce the heat to medium and cook the apples, stirring occasionally, until they are just soft, about 5 minutes. Set aside and keep warm while you prepare the pancake batter and preheat the broiler.

In a 10-inch ovenproof skillet, cook 1 pancake as directed in the pancake recipe above until the bottom of the pancake is lightly browned and the batter has begun to firm up. Arrange 4 of the sausage patties and $^1/_2$ of the cooked apples over the top of the pancake. Place the skillet 4 to 5 inches away from the heat and broil until the top is browned and the center is just set, but still soft, 4 to 5 minutes. Cut into 4 wedges, garnish with powdered sugar and cinnamon, and serve; then cook the other pancake.

Makes two 10-inch pancakes, serves 4.

Mediterranean Sausage Puffy Pancakes

T hese savory pancakes are wonderful for a brunch, lunch, or light dinner. The trick is to omit the sugar from the recipe and only broil the pancake for three minutes or so since these savory varieties cook quicker than sweet ones.

2 teaspoons butter
$^1/_2$ pound Mediterranean Sausage (page 24), formed into
    8 patties
1 recipe Bette's Puffy Pancakes (page 73), without sugar
    or cinnamon

1 cup shredded Swiss cheese
$^1/_2$ cup pitted and chopped Greek olives
Pitted Greek olives for garnish

Melt the butter in a heavy skillet and fry the sausage patties over medium-high heat, turning once until they are lightly browned on both sides, about 7 minutes total. Remove from skillet and set aside.

Preheat the broiler. Prepare the pancake batter omitting the sugar and cinnamon. Just before you fold in the egg whites, stir in the shredded cheese and chopped olives.

In a 10-inch ovenproof skillet, cook 1 pancake as directed in pancake recipe until the bottom is lightly browned and the batter has begun to firm up. Arrange 4 of the sausage patties over the top of the pancake. Place the skillet in the broiler, 4 to 5 inches away from the heat and broil until the top is browned and the center is just set, but still soft, about 3 minutes. Garnish with Greek olives, cut the pancake into 4 wedges, and serve; then cook the other pancake.

Makes two 10-inch pancakes, serves 4.

Chinese Black Mushroom Sausage Puffy Pancakes

These unusual and very tasty pancakes make a great lunch when served with our Chinese Salad with Ginger Orange Dressing (page 125).

---

2 teaspoons butter
½ pound Chinese Black Mushroom Sausage (page 26), formed into 8 patties
1 recipe Bette's Puffy Pancakes (page 73), without sugar or cinnamon
¾ cup thinly sliced green onions, white and green parts

½ cup chopped bamboo shoots*
½ cup fresh bean sprouts
Chopped green onions, soy sauce, and Asian sesame oil* for garnish

* See Glossary

Melt the butter in a heavy skillet and fry the sausage patties over medium-high heat, turning once until they are lightly browned on both sides, about 7 minutes total.

Preheat the broiler. Prepare the pancake batter, omitting the sugar and cinnamon. Just before you fold in the egg whites, stir in half the sliced green onions, chopped bamboo shoots, and fresh bean sprouts.

In a 10-inch ovenproof skillet, cook 1 pancake as described in the pancake recipe until the bottom is lightly browned and the batter has begun to firm up. Arrange 4 of the sausage patties over the top of the pancake. Place the skillet in the broiler 4 to 5 inches away from the heat and broil until the top is browned and the center is just set, but still soft, about 3 minutes. Garnish with chopped green onions, sprinkle with soy sauce and sesame oil, and cut into 4 wedges; then cook the other pancake.

Makes two 10-inch pancakes, serves 4.

The variations of puffy pancakes topped with spicy sausage are endless. Try the following combinations out on family and friends and then invent your own toppings and batter additions.

- Spicy Louisiana Sausage (page 18) with chopped red pepper as topping; chopped green onions, dash each Worcestershire sauce and Tabasco in the batter.
- Thai Chicken and Turkey Sausage (page 28) with chopped basil as topping; chopped cilantro, green chiles* in the batter.
- Southwest Green Chile Sausage (page 20) as topping; chopped chipotle chiles,* green chiles* in the batter.

* See Glossary

BETTE'S PERFECT PANCAKE TIPS

Ever wonder why most pancake recipes say, "Do not overmix"?

Overmixing a pancake batter develops the glutens and makes the resulting pancakes tough and rubbery just like those we all remember from summer camp. Overmixing also pops the air bubbles that make for light and airy cakes. The trick is to mix the dry ingredients thoroughly in a separate bowl. This way you won't need to do much further mixing once the wet ingredients are added. Mix the wet ingredients together in a separate large bowl. Always start by first beating the eggs lightly and then adding the other liquids and melted butter, if used. Then you should add *all* the dry ingredients *at once* to the bowl of wet ingredients. Gently stir the batter just enough to moisten all the dry ingredients. Don't worry about little lumps because they will cook out and disappear.

Bette's Diner Corn Cakes

Bette Kroening and Sue Farley are two of the original partners of thirteen-year-old Bette's Diner in Berkeley, which is known nationwide for its fantastic breakfasts. Although their buttermilk pancakes and buckwheat pancakes are classics, these corn cakes have always been among our favorites. They are delicious as is, but also they are wonderfully easy to embellish and turn into satisfying sausage dishes. Bette has served these delectable corn cakes to her delighted patrons over the years (former Senator Jacob Javits was a special aficionado of the crisp cakes). She has also recently packaged the mix for home use. It is available from specialty food stores or direct from Bette's (see Sources, page 224).

2 cups water
2 tablespoons butter
$^1/_4$ teaspoon salt
1 tablespoon sugar
1 cup yellow cornmeal
2 eggs

$^1/_2$ cup milk
$^1/_4$ cup stone-ground whole wheat flour or all-purpose flour
$^1/_4$ cup cake flour
2 teaspoons baking powder
Butter, berry or maple syrup, and warmed honey
    for accompaniments

In a small saucepan, bring the water and butter to a boil. Stir in the salt and sugar and pour over the cornmeal in a large bowl. Stir to combine and thoroughly moisten the cornmeal. Cover and let the mixture rest for 10 minutes.

In another bowl, lightly beat the eggs, stir in the milk, and quickly mix in both flours and baking powder. *Do not overmix.* Add the egg-flour mixture to the cornmeal and stir just enough to combine.

Heat a lightly oiled griddle or heavy skillet over medium-high heat. Pour $^1/_4$ cup of batter onto the hot surface to form a 4- to 5-inch cake. Cook 3 or 4 cakes at a time, being sure not to crowd them. When bubbles come to the surface of the pancake and the underside is lightly browned, turn and cook for an additional 2 to 3 minutes, until the other side is lightly browned. Serve with butter, syrup, or warmed honey.

Makes 16 small pancakes, serves 2 to 4.

Spicy Louisiana Sausage Corn Cakes

These spicy cakes can be enjoyed for brunch or lunch with our Southwest Black Bean Salad (page 114) or for dinner with our Creole Turkey Grillades (page 169). Two or three pancakes make an ample portion as a side dish. They are also excellent with pork chops, chicken, or shrimp.

2 teaspoons vegetable oil
½ pound Spicy Louisiana Sausage (page 18)
1 recipe Bette's Diner Corn Cakes (page 78)
½ cup uncooked sweet corn kernels (fresh or frozen)

¼ cup chopped, seeded, and deveined red bell pepper (optional)
½ cup chopped green onions, white and green parts

Heat the oil in a skillet over medium-high heat and fry the sausage for 3 to 4 minutes, breaking it up as it cooks. Remove with a slotted spoon and reserve.

Prepare the corn cake batter as directed, and mix in the cooked sausage, corn, bell pepper (if using), and green onions. Cook as directed in corn cake recipe, making three 4- to 5-inch cakes at a time.

Makes 16 small pancakes, serves 6 to 8 as a side dish, 4 as a main course.

Tex-Mex Mini Corn Cakes

T hese fiery, bite-sized corn cakes make terrific appetizers or party snacks, when paired with a full-bodied amber lager like Dos Equis or Beck's Oktoberfest. For a substantial brunch or a light dinner make the corn cakes larger (4 to 5 inches), and serve with our Southwest Green Chile Sausage and Cabbage Salad (page 115).

---

1 pound Southwest Green Chile Sausage (page 20)
1 tablespoon vegetable oil
1 recipe Bette's Diner Corn Cakes (page 78)
1/2 cup uncooked sweet corn kernels (fresh or frozen)
1/2 cup canned diced mild green chiles*

1 cup shredded Cheddar or jack cheese
Salsa Cruda (page 213) and Chipotle Sour Cream
    (page 212) for garnish

* See Glossary

For mini cakes, form sausage into 32 patties, 2 to 2 1/2 inches in diameter; for larger cakes, form into 16 patties, 4 to 5 inches in diameter. Put the oil in a skillet over medium-high heat and panfry the sausage patties on both sides until done, about 7 minutes total. Remove from pan and keep warm.

Prepare the batter for corn cakes and stir in the corn and chiles before cooking cakes. Follow the directions in corn cake recipe for cooking cakes, except use only half as much batter (2 tablespoons) for the mini cake, and once the cakes are turned, mound the cooked side of each with shredded cheese. When the underside is done and the cheese melted, arrange the corn cakes on a serving platter. Top each cake with a cooked sausage patty. Garnish with fresh Salsa Cruda and Chipotle Sour Cream.

Makes 32 mini pancakes or 16 pancakes, serves 8 to 10 as appetizers, 4 as brunch or main course.

Thai Shrimp Salad Corn Cakes

 he combination of these crunchy corn cakes with the bright, fresh flavors of our Thai Shrimp salad is simply irresistible. For a memorable brunch—or even lunch or dinner—pair the shrimp-topped cakes with our Ginger Orange Slaw (page 62).

---

1 recipe Bette's Diner Corn Cakes (page 78)
1 tablespoon chopped fresh cilantro
1/2 cup uncooked sweet corn kernels (fresh or frozen)

Thai Shrimp Salad
1 tablespoon peanut oil
1/2 pound Thai Chicken and Turkey Sausage (page 28)
1 cup diced raw shrimp (about 1/2 pound shelled shrimp)

1 avocado, peeled and diced
1 cup finely diced unpeeled cucumber
1 cup diced ripe tomato
4 to 5 tablespoons fresh lime juice
Dash or 2 Tabasco
2 tablespoons chopped fresh mint
Salt and freshly ground black pepper to taste

Prepare corn cake batter and add the chopped cilantro and corn. Cook 4-inch cakes as directed in recipe, and set aside.

To make the shrimp salad: Heat the oil in a large skillet or wok over medium-high heat and fry the sausage, breaking it up as it cooks, for 5 minutes. Add the shrimp and stir-fry until pink and firm, about 5 minutes. Transfer this mixture to a bowl and mix with the remaining ingredients. Taste for salt and pepper. Place 2 corn cakes on each plate and top with the shrimp salad.

Serves 6 to 8 as a side dish or first course, 4 as a main course.

Cafe Beaujolais Yogurt Pancakes with Sausage and Apples

Margaret Fox, chef/owner of Cafe Beaujolais, is our other West Coast pancake queen. Her version of tangy yogurt pancakes was developed at our request as a low-fat alternative to the classic buttermilk pancake to serve with our sausages. Margaret and husband chef/owner Chris Kumpf are known for more than just pancakes, though. Lunches and dinners at Cafe Beaujolais in the windswept seaside town of Mendocino draw enthusiastic diners from up and down the coast. And Margaret and Chris also offer a full line of imaginative baked goods, pancake mixes, and other fine products at the restaurant and through mail order (see Sources, page 224). Obviously breakfast is well taken care of at the cafe. After some some pleasant experiments, they devised this recipe to be served with Chicken and Apple Sausage patties and sautéed apple slices. Chris also suggests fresh berries and a dollop of yogurt as an accompaniment to the flavorful pancakes.

2 teaspoons butter
1/2 pound Chicken and Apple Sausage (page 16), formed
  into 8 patties
1 cup peeled, cored, and sliced apples (about 1 medium apple)
1/4 teaspoon ground cinnamon
1 tablespoon sugar

Yogurt Pancakes
1 1/2 cups all-purpose flour
1 1/2 tablespoons sugar
1 teaspoon salt
1 1/2 teaspoons baking powder
1 teaspoon baking soda
2 eggs
2 cups plain low-fat yogurt
1/4 cup canola oil, plus a little oil for skillet
3 tablespoons cold water

Put the butter in a heavy skillet and fry the sausage patties over medium-high heat, turning once, until lightly browned on both sides, about 7 minutes total. Remove and reserve patties. Add the apples to the skillet and sprinkle with the cinnamon and sugar. Reduce the heat to medium and cook the apples, stirring occasionally, until they are just soft, about 5 minutes. Set aside and keep warm while you prepare the pancakes.

Sift together the flour, sugar, salt, baking powder, and baking soda into a mixing bowl. In a separate bowl, whisk together the remaining ingredients and add to the dry mixture, stirring lightly to blend.

Heat a lightly oiled griddle or heavy skillet over medium-high heat. Pour 1/4 cup of the batter onto the hot surface to form a pancake. Cook 3 or 4 cakes at a time, making sure not to crowd them. When bubbles come to the surface of the pancake and the underside is lightly browned, flip the cake and cook until the other side is lightly browned, 2 to 3 minutes. Remove pancakes as they cook and reserve.

Spread 3 to 4 pancakes on each plate. Spoon sautéed apples over the pancakes along with a bit of the juice and top each portion with 2 cooked sausage patties. Serve at once.

Makes 12 to 16 pancakes, serves 4.

French Toast Stuffed with Chicken and Apple Sausage

French toast and sausage patties are an American tradition that has fallen out of favor, since pork sausage is considered too fatty in these health-conscious days. But with our Chicken and Apple Sausage you can still have the old-fashioned flavor without worrying so much. Stuffed French toast makes a satisfying and guilt-free breakfast. It is basically a French toast sandwich stuffed with lightly browned Chicken and Apple Sausage patties and topped with sautéed apples in an apple cider syrup. Just as delicious as the classic combo, but a bit lighter and healthier.

---

3 eggs
2 cups milk
1 tablespoon ground cinnamon
1 teaspoon ground nutmeg
8 slices French bread or egg bread

2 tablespoons butter
1 pound Chicken and Apple Sausage (page 16), formed into
  8 patties
Sautéed Apple Slices (following)

Whisk together the eggs, milk, cinnamon, and nutmeg in a large bowl. Soak the bread slices in the egg mixture. Melt the butter on a griddle or nonstick skillet, and fry the bread slices over medium-high heat, turning once or twice, until nicely browned. Cover and keep warm.

In a large nonstick skillet, panfry the sausage patties over medium heat for 6 to 7 minutes, turning once or twice. Cut into a patty to test for doneness; there should be no pink showing. Cover and keep warm while you sauté the apples.

Place 1 slice of French toast on each plate and coat it with apples and their syrup. Cover with 2 patties of cooked sausage. Cover the patties with the second piece of French toast, and spoon more apples and syrup over the top.

Serves 4.

Sautéed Apple Slices

Our favorite apple for this dish is a firm, tart apple such as Granny Smith or pippin. The sautéed apples are also delightful on pancakes and waffles, with grilled pork chops or sausages, or as an accompaniment to baked ham. They also make a great topping for ice cream. The apples in syrup will keep, covered in the refrigerator, for a week to ten days. They also freeze well.

4 cups sliced, peeled, and cored apples (Granny Smith or pippin)
1 tablespoon butter

3 cups apple cider
Pinch ground cloves

In a skillet, sauté the apples in the butter over medium heat until slightly soft, about 3 minutes. Add the cider and cloves and boil over high heat until the apples and cider form a thick syrup.

Makes about 4 cups.

Waffles of Yore: A Knight's Tale

According to medieval lore, the first waffles were produced when the gallant knight, Sir Giles, inadvertently sat down on his wife's oat cakes while wearing his chain-mail armor. Famished after a day of jousting and bashing his fellow knights, Sir Giles was undaunted by this minor mishap. He spread the flattened and dented cakes with sweet butter, not even offering a bite to his good wife Ermenetrude. Surprisingly, he found the cakes especially delicious—the indentations caused by his armor kept the butter from running off the cake.

When Sir Giles shared his discovery, the cakes proved so popular that he was asked week after week to put on his armor and sit on the cakes. Eventually somebody came up with the idea of the waffle iron, thereby sparing Sir Giles and all other husbands to follow the onerous task of putting on armor every Sunday morning. We found this enchanting tale in *The Gold Book* by Louis de Gouy. He also tells us that the word "waffle" evolved because it was easy to say when your mouth is full, a necessity when calling out for more waffles.

Waffles, whatever their origin, first found their way into American cooking in tea rooms in the deep South as a savory accompaniment to fried chicken. These early waffles were probably made from sweet potatoes or yams as well as corn or wheat flour. We don't know who first realized that waffles spread with butter and maple syrup made an awfully fine breakfast, but the concept has certainly lasted. Recently with the awakened interest in American regional cooking, waffles have again appeared as a savory used in appetizers or as side dishes with the main course. And any way you eat them, waffles and sausage are a great combination—for breakfast, lunch or even dinner.

Marion Cunningham's Raised Waffles

This recipe makes the best waffles either of us have ever eaten—light, crisp, and slightly tangy. They are a great foil for savory ingredients such as smoked salmon or crab salad and we have used them as a base for several sausage recipes. More traditionally they could be served with syrup or fresh fruit. We think these waffles are also delicious with fried patties of our Chicken and Apple Sausage (page 16) or as a side dish with Stuffed Pork Chops with Gorgonzola and Sun-Dried Tomatoes (page 173) or Creole Turkey Grillades (page 169). The recipe originally appeared in the *Fannie Farmer Boston Cookbook* and was adapted by Marion Cunningham in *The Breakfast Book*. Bruce's wife, Nancy Oakes, has further adapted it for her San Francisco restaurant, Boulevard, where she serves the waffles with a variety of savory ingredients. Note that this yeast batter must rise in the refrigerator overnight.

1/2 cup lukewarm water
1 package active dry yeast
2 cups milk, warmed
1 stick (1/4 pound) butter, melted
1 teaspoon salt

1 teaspoon sugar
1 cup yellow cornmeal
1 cup all-purpose flour
2 eggs, lightly beaten
1/4 teaspoon baking powder

Put the warm water in a large bowl, sprinkle on the yeast, and let stand 5 minutes to activate and dissolve the yeast. Add the remaining ingredients, except the baking powder. Beat the batter until smooth and well blended, transfer to a large storage container (when the batter is added, the container should only be half full), cover, and refrigerate overnight. The batter will rise in the refrigerator and almost double in size.

Just prior to baking the waffles, remove the batter from the refrigerator. Stir in the baking powder and any of the ingredients called for in the following recipes, if using. (The batter is quite thin compared to conventional waffle batters.) Preheat the waffle iron. Pour in enough batter just to cover the bottom of the waffle iron, about 1/2 to 3/4 cup, depending on the size of your iron. Close the iron, and cook until the waffles are golden brown and crisp. The batter will keep for 2 to 3 days in the refrigerator.

Makes 6 to 8 waffles.

Chicken and Apple Sausage Waffles

or a simple, but elegant brunch serve the waffles with chunky applesauce or a sweet fruit chutney; for lunch accompany them with yogurt or sour cream and Nancy's Corn Relish (page 208).

2 teaspoons vegetable oil
¹/₂ pound Chicken and Apple Sausage (page 16)

1 recipe Marion Cunningham's Raised Waffles (page 87)

Heat the oil in a skillet over medium-high heat and panfry the sausage for 3 to 4 minutes, breaking it up as it cooks. Add the cooked sausage to the finished waffle batter and bake as directed in the waffle recipe.

Serves 4 as a main course, 8 as an appetizer.

Italian Sausage Waffles with Fresh Tomato and Basil Sauce

This spicy, Italian-accented waffle makes an unusual and delicious main course for brunch, lunch, or a light dinner accompanied with our Italian Sausage and Spinach Salad with Polenta Croutons (page 116). It also serves as a colorful first course or appetizer for an Italian feast or buffet.

---

2 teaspoons olive oil
1/2 pound Italian Turkey and Sun-Dried Tomato Sausage
   (page 22) or other good-quality Italian sausage

1/2 cup freshly grated Parmesan cheese, plus more for topping
1 recipe Marion Cunningham's Raised Waffles (page 87)
2 cups Fresh Tomato and Basil Sauce (page 145)

Heat the oil in a skillet over medium-high heat and panfry the sausage for 3 to 4 minutes, breaking it up as it cooks. Add the cooked sausage and grated cheese to the finished waffle batter and bake as directed in the waffle recipe.

Serve with Fresh Tomato and Basil Sauce and more grated Parmesan cheese.

Serves 4 as a main course, 8 as a first course or appetizer.

Soups

Soups

Soups are typical of the generous, hearty, and nutritious foods that make country cooking so satisfying. Soups also provide a lot of nourishment for little money, and they don't have to be high in fat or calories.

With a few vegetables, some dried beans or lentils, and an assortment of our tasty sausages in the freezer, you can turn out delicious soups quickly and with very little effort. Each sausage gives a soup its own flavor profile: All you have to do is fry up a little sausage, add some onions, carrots, celery, a cup of precooked or canned beans, some homemade or canned stock, and within forty-five minutes you can call out "Soup's on!" and watch the family come running.

Some of the soups in this chapter are somewhat more involved, such as our Gourmet Gulch Chicken Chowder (page 94) and Southwest Tomatillo Soup (page 97), but none requires complicated procedures or long, drawn-out cooking. A plus is that many soups like our San Francisco Minestrone (page 100), Tuscan Bean Soup (page 101), and Spicy Hungarian Goulash Soup (page 106) improve with a day or two of aging in the refrigerator. Thus you can let them cook on Sunday while you are reading the paper on the deck. Then heat them up later in the week for delicious and quick dinners.

Homemade Stock

In most of our recipes you can use canned stock (low-sodium preferred), but making your own chicken, turkey, or beef stock doesn't have to take a lot of time and effort. The results are certainly better than canned stocks, and you can use up leftovers and scraps from the fridge. Use the basic ratio below of about 2 pounds of bones and meat scraps to 1½ quarts (6 cups) of water, make up as much stock as you wish at a time, and freeze for later use. We suggest that you don't salt the stock until you use it in a soup or other dish.

---

2 pounds chicken, turkey, beef, or veal bones and scraps,
    raw or cooked (for richer stock use chicken backs, necks,
    and wings or beef shank)
1½ quarts (6 cups) cold water
1 onion, chopped

1 carrot, chopped
1 rib celery, chopped
1 sprig fresh thyme or 1 teaspoon dried thyme
1 bay leaf
4 black peppercorns

If using raw bones and scraps, preheat the oven to 400°F, and roast for 10 minutes for more color and flavor. Cover with water in a large pot, and bring to a boil. Skim and discard any foam, add remaining ingredients, lower heat and simmer uncovered for 1½ to 2 hours. Strain, and cool overnight in refrigerator. Remove congealed fat before using or freezing.

Makes 4 to 5 cups.

Berkeley's Gourmet Gulch

It all started in the mid-1960s with Peet's Coffee on Vine near Shattuck in Berkeley, a hotbed of French-roast beans and frenzied attempts to save the world through conversation by the coffee crazies gathered around the espresso machine. This was soon followed by the Cheese Board, a co-op of earnest cheese fanciers that turned on a whole generation of Berkeleyites to the pleasures of triple crème and chèvre. Then came Chez Panisse, at first a group of Francophile grad students in a funky turn-of-the-century house cooking dishes that reminded them of that glorious year abroad. A bakery devoted to the needs of chocoholics, Cocolat, soon appeared, along with America's first charcuterie, Pig by the Tail, and all of a sudden a sleepy stretch of Shattuck Avenue became the Gourmet Ghetto, an area that today is world renowned for innovative and delicious food, the birthplace of "California Cuisine."

One of the early shops in the Gourmet Ghetto was Poulet, a combination deli and restaurant that specialized in chicken cooked every which way: in salads, entrées, sandwiches, pastas, soups, pâtés, what you will. This is where Bruce began his cooking career as head chef and creative chicken plucker. In addition to supplying the bustling takeout counter, he prepared delicious lunches and light dinners every day consisting of a main dish and a constantly revolving selection of wonderful soups.

Gourmet Gulch Chicken Chowder

BRUCE SAYS

"ONE OF THE MOST POPULAR SOUPS THAT I COOKED AT POULET WAS THIS CHICKEN CHOWDER MADE WITH CHICKEN AND APPLE SAUSAGE, COOKED CHICKEN OR TURKEY, AND BACON. THIS RECIPE MAKES A FULL POT OF SOUP THAT WILL EASILY FEED A WHOLE COUCHFUL OF SUPER BOWL WARRIORS OR ALL THOSE HOUSE GUESTS WHO PARTIED A BIT TOO LONG THE NIGHT BEFORE. LEFTOVERS ARE A GODSEND SINCE THE SOUP IS EVEN BETTER REWARMED."

2 slices bacon, cut into small strips
$1/2$ pound Chicken and Apple Sausage (page 16)
1 onion, coarsely chopped
2 leeks, whites only, thinly sliced
1 carrot, diced
2 ribs celery, diced
$1/4$ cup all-purpose flour

1 pound unpeeled white or red new potatoes, diced
2 quarts rich chicken stock, preferably homemade (page 92)
1 cup white wine
2 cups diced cooked chicken or turkey
2 cups half-and-half
Salt and freshly ground black pepper to taste
Chopped fresh parsley for garnish

Brown the bacon in a heavy soup pot over medium-high heat. Remove with a slotted spoon and reserve. Add the sausage and fry for 5 minutes, breaking it apart as it cooks. Remove and reserve.

In the same pot over medium heat, cook the onion, leeks, carrot, and celery until the vegetables are soft, about 10 minutes. Sprinkle the flour over the vegetables, stir well, and cook for an additional 2 minutes, stirring often. Add the diced potato and stir well to coat with the vegetable-flour mixture.

Remove the pot from the heat and gradually stir in the stock and wine, stirring briskly to avoid lumps. Cook the chowder at a simmer for 45 minutes, stirring occasionally. Ten minutes before serving, add the diced chicken, reserved bacon and sausage, and the half-and-half. Taste for salt and pepper. Garnish with chopped parsley.

Serves 6 to 8.

Creole Corn and Seafood Chowder

As with all dishes made with fresh corn, this chowder is best when the corn is freshly picked and at its sweetest. Happily some new varieties developed recently hold their sweetness for quite a while after picking. In a pinch you could use frozen corn, but the results are never quite as good. Just about any seafood is delicious in this light and spicy soup. Our preference is for cooked lobster or crab, but you could also use raw shrimp or scallops (add two to three minutes to the cooking time for raw ingredients).

6 ears fresh sweet corn (3 to 4 cups of kernels)
4 cups chicken stock, preferably homemade (page 92)
1 tablespoon butter
½ pound Spicy Louisiana Sausage (page 18)
1 teaspoon salt
½ teaspoon sugar
4 cups whole milk

1 tablespoon cornstarch dissolved in 2 tablespoons water or milk
4 green onions, white and green parts, finely chopped
2 cups seafood (such as cooked lobster, cooked crab, diced raw shrimp, diced raw scallops)
Salt and freshly ground black pepper
Tabasco (optional)

Husk and wash corn. Using a sharp knife slice the kernels from the cobs from the top of the ear downward. Do not cut too close to the cob. Set kernels aside in a bowl.

Put the cobs in a large pot, cover with the stock, and bring to a boil. Reduce heat to a simmer, cover, and cook cobs for 30 to 40 minutes. Remove the cobs and reserve cobs and stock.

In a large soup pot or Dutch oven, heat the butter over medium-high heat. Add the sausage and fry for 5 minutes, breaking it up as it cooks. Add the stock, salt, sugar, milk, and corn kernels and bring to a simmer. Using a spoon or the back of a knife, scrape any pulp from the cobs into the soup. Stir in the dissolved cornstarch and cook until the soup thickens slightly, 2 to 3 minutes. Stir in the green onions and seafood and cook 5 more minutes (7 to 8 minutes if using raw seafood). Taste seafood once or twice to be sure it is not being overcooked. Taste for salt and pepper. Put in a couple of dashes of Tabasco if you like a spicier chowder. Ladle into bowls and serve at once.

Serves 6 to 8.

Eggplant Gumbo

This unusual gumbo of okra and eggplant originated at Corine Dunbar's, one of New Orleans's great Creole restaurants. Our version comes from Tom Blower, a Creole chef who adapted it while cooking in Los Angeles. If fresh okra is unavailable, frozen will do just as well.

4 tablespoons olive oil
1/2 pound Spicy Louisiana Sausage (page 18)
1 large eggplant (about 1 1/2 pounds), peeled and diced
3 cups diced onion
1 cup diced celery
2 tablespoons minced garlic

1 can (28 ounces) Italian-style tomatoes, chopped, and drained
2 red or green bell peppers or a mixture, seeded, deveined, and diced
1/2 pound okra, sliced
6 cups chicken stock, preferably homemade (page 92)
Salt, freshly ground black pepper, and sugar to taste

In a large soup pot or Dutch oven, heat 1 tablespoon of the oil over medium-high heat. Fry the sausage for 5 minutes, breaking it apart as it cooks. Remove 2/3 of the sausage and reserve. Add 2 tablespoons of the remaining oil and cook the eggplant over medium heat until soft, about 10 minutes. Remove sausage and eggplant, and reserve.

Put the final tablespoon of oil in the pan and slowly cook the onions, celery, and garlic over medium heat, stirring frequently. Return the eggplant and sausage mixture to the pot along with the tomatoes, bell peppers, okra, and chicken stock. Add a pinch of salt and pepper and cook uncovered at a simmer for about 1 hour. Return the reserved sausage to the pot, and cook 10 minutes more. Taste for salt and pepper and add a pinch of sugar if desired. Serve at once. Or cover and refrigerate to reheat and serve the next day.

Serves 6 to 8.

Southwest Tomatillo Soup

Tomatillos, also called "ground cherries," look like little green tomatoes with husks, but are actually related to Cape gooseberries. They have a refreshing, tart flavor, more like sour cherries than tomatoes. Fresh tomatillos, usually available in Latino markets, are preferable, but canned tomatillos also work well. This lively soup was inspired by a recipe from Amey Shaw, who used to cook great Southwestern food at the now-defunct Fourth Street Grill in Berkeley and is one of the San Francisco Bay Area's finest and most versatile chefs. You can substitute canned Ortega brand chiles for the fresh, if you like.

1 tablespoon olive oil
1 pound Southwest Green Chile Sausage (page 20)
2 cups chopped onions
¼ cup minced garlic
3 to 4 cups chicken stock, preferably homemade (page 92)
4 mild green chiles* (such as Anaheim* or poblano*) or
   2 green bell peppers, fire-roasted (page 20), peeled, and
   cut into thin strips
12 fresh or canned tomatillos, husked and diced
3 ripe tomatoes, peeled, seeded, and diced

2 bunches (4 to 6 ounces each) cilantro, washed and tied
   with a string
Juice of 1 lime
Salt and freshly ground black pepper to taste
2 corn tortillas, cut into strips
Vegetable oil for frying
1 cup freshly shredded jack cheese or queso fresco*
Chopped fresh cilantro for garnish

* See Glossary

Heat the oil in a large soup pot or Dutch oven over medium-high heat and fry the sausage for 5 minutes, breaking it up as it cooks. Add the onions and garlic and fry for 7 minutes more, stirring frequently. Put in the chicken stock and bring to a boil. Reduce to a simmer and add the chiles or peppers, tomatillos, tomatoes, and tied cilantro bunches. Cook for 30 minutes. Season with lime juice and taste for salt and pepper. In a heavy saucepan, heat 2 to 3 inches of oil until very hot over high heat, and deep-fry the tortilla strips until crisp. Remove and drain on paper towels.

To serve the soup, remove and discard the cilantro bunches and ladle the soup into serving bowls. Garnish with shredded cheese, tortilla strips, and chopped cilantro.

Serves 4 to 6.

Lentil Soup South American Style

Cilantro's tangy, pungent character adds a wonderful accent to the lentils in this spicy soup. The recipe works just as well with split peas or black beans. Split peas will require about the same cooking time as lentils, while black beans may require an hour or so of extra cooking (see Lalime's Black Beans, page 196). Vegetables are added twice: first to flavor the lentils and later to provide the fresh taste and texture of the vegetables themselves.

1 tablespoon olive oil
1 pound Southwest Green Chile Sausage (page 20)
3 quarts chicken stock, preferably homemade (page 92)
    or water
2 cups brown lentils
2 bay leaves
4 carrots, chopped
3 ribs celery, chopped

1 large onion, chopped
1 bunch (4 to 6 ounces) cilantro
6 green onions, white and green parts, chopped
Salt and freshly ground black pepper to taste

Plain yogurt or sour cream (optional)
Salsa Cruda (page 213)
Chopped fresh cilantro

Heat the oil in a large soup pot or Dutch oven over medium-high heat and fry the sausage for 5 minutes, breaking it up as it cooks. Remove $^2/_3$ of the sausage and reserve. Add the chicken stock, lentils, bay leaves, $^1/_2$ of the chopped carrots, $^1/_2$ of the celery, and all the onions to the remaining sausage in the pot. Bring to a boil and reduce to a simmer.

Finely chop the cilantro stems and coarsely chop the leaves. Add the chopped stems to the pot. Cook for 30 minutes or until the lentils are just tender. Add the remaining carrots and celery and cook for 15 minutes. Put in the reserved sausage, the green onions, and all but 2 tablespoons of the cilantro leaves. Cook soup 10 minutes more. Taste for salt and pepper.

Ladle into bowls. Garnish with a dollop of yogurt or sour cream, if using, a spoonful of Salsa Cruda, and a scattering of chopped cilantro.

Serves 6 to 8.

Soup's On (and On and On) in North Beach Kitchens

A few years back, the North Beach section of San Francisco was peppered with old-fashioned, family-style Italian restaurants. Some survive today, although the prices have gone up a bit over the years. But you can still get a hearty, rib-sticking four- or five-course meal that any Italian-American mama would be proud to serve, and all for very little money. Hungry college students continue to line up in front of the more popular restaurants on Friday nights, and harried families bring the kids to fill up on minestrone and pasta. Everybody's friendly, the conversation is lively, the food is delicious, the wine is cheap and good, and a merry time is had by all.

The format hasn't varied over the years. First comes the antipasto platter of salami, mortadella, provolone, pickled peppers, and raw vegetables. Then a huge bowl of steaming minestrone arrives at the table. And it's always the same minestrone—thick and flavorful, redolent of garlic and herbs. The guess is that there is a perpetual pot of soup living forever on the back of the stove in each of these kitchens. And every day some beans, vegetables, ham, and sausage are added. If the soup gets too thick, a little stock is poured in to make it almost liquid again. Always changing, but always the same, this minestrone just tastes good. Too good, really, because the trick is not to fill up on this virtually unlimited and seemingly immortal soup, since the rest of the meal is still to come: ravioli or spaghetti, chicken cacciatore or roast beef along with roast potatoes and chard or spinach with garlic and oil. And at the end of the meal, always spumoni ice cream, gobbled up by the kids, with maybe an espresso and a small glass of grappa for the old folks.

San Francisco Minestrone

That thick and long-lived minestrone was just a single course back when we were starving students. But these days we think that the minestrone is enough for the whole meal. Accompanied by some crusty sourdough and a glass of Chianti or Zinfandel, a bowl of this thick and flavorful soup is just the thing for a winter dinner. Be sure to make the soup the day before you are going to serve it. The flavors come together nicely and the minestrone gets that rich, old-fashioned character we all love.

2 to 3 quarts chicken or beef stock, preferably homemade (page 92)
1 cup dried white navy beans, soaked overnight in cold water to cover
½ cup brown lentils
2 cups chopped Italian-style canned tomatoes, with liquid
½ pound Italian Turkey and Sun-Dried Tomato Sausage (page 22), formed into small meatballs
½ cup chopped carrots

½ cup chopped celery
1 cup chopped onions
2 bunches (12 ounces each) spinach, washed and chopped
½ small cabbage, thinly sliced
3 cups diced zucchini, pattypan, or yellow crookneck squash
1 cup dried elbow macaroni
Salt and freshly ground black pepper to taste
Freshly grated Parmesan cheese for garnish

In a large soup pot, bring the stock to a boil. Drain the beans and add to the stock. Reduce the heat to a simmer and cook until the beans are just tender, 1½ to 2 hours. Add the lentils and cook for 20 minutes more. Put in the tomatoes, sausage meatballs, carrots, celery, and onions. Cook for 20 minutes more. Add the spinach, cabbage, squash, and macaroni. Cook until the pasta is tender, 10 to 15 minutes. Taste for salt and pepper.

The soup is best cooked, refrigerated overnight, and then reheated the next day, but you can serve it right from the stove. Either way, serve it with a generous sprinkle of freshly grated Parmesan cheese.

Serves 8 to 10.

Tuscan Bean Soup

Beans are an important part of the Italian diet, particularly in Tuscany where they are often paired with fresh vegetables, herbs, and sausages. Beans come in all kinds of shapes, colors, and flavors, but they are all healthy and nourishing. High in fiber and carbohydrates and low in calories and fat, they are a welcome addition to a health-giving diet. But beans alone can be a bit bland. The key to healthful cooking with beans is not to load them up with too much fat in the quest for flavor. Our poultry-based sausages are ideal here. Just a little bit of these "flavor bombs" added to beans along with some fresh vegetables and herbs can give you delicious bean dishes without high levels of fat, but with plenty of flavor. One of the best ways to eat beans is in soup. This Tuscan-style bean soup makes a hearty addition to the winter table.

1 pound dried white beans (Great Northern, navy, cannellini), soaked overnight in water to cover, and drained

2 quarts chicken stock, preferably homemade (page 92)

1 tablespoon olive oil

1 pound Italian Turkey and Sun-Dried Tomato Sausage (page 22)

1 1/2 pounds beets, peeled and chopped, with green tops, cleaned and chopped

3 fresh or canned Italian-style tomatoes, chopped and drained

2 ribs celery, chopped

4 carrots, chopped

2 medium onions, chopped

4 sprigs fresh rosemary or 1 teaspoon dried rosemary

2 garlic cloves, chopped

Salt and freshly ground black pepper to taste

Garnish

8 slices French bread

Olive oil

Freshly grated Parmesan cheese

Drain the presoaked beans and put in a large soup pot. Add the chicken stock and bring to a boil. In a skillet, panfry the sausage in 1 tablespoon of olive oil for 4 to 5 minutes over medium heat, breaking it up as it cooks. Add 1/2 of the cooked sausage to the beans, lower the heat, and simmer slowly for 1 hour, uncovered. Put in the vegetables, rosemary, and garlic, and cook until the beans are tender, 30 minutes to 1 hour. Add the remaining sausage and cook for 5 minutes more. Taste for salt and pepper.

About 1/2 hour before the beans are ready, preheat the oven to 350°F. Drizzle the bread slices with olive oil and sprinkle generously with grated Parmesan. Bake on an oiled cookie sheet until the bread is crisp and the cheese browned, 12 to 15 minutes. Ladle soup into bowls and garnish with the cheese toasts.

Serves 6 to 8.

Italian Sausage Soup

One of the glories of Italian cooking lies in its combination of simplicity with intense flavors. Richly spiced sausages, powerful cheeses, and fresh vegetables and herbs are often combined with beans, pasta, or rice to provide dishes that are simple and healthy, yet full of flavor. In this delicious soup most of the flavor comes from the sausage. We used our Italian Turkey and Sun-Dried Tomato Sausage, but any high-quality Italian sausage will do. Use fresh Italian-style (Roma) tomatoes or canned plum tomatoes, domestic or—even better—imported from Italy. And try to use the true imported Parmagiano Reggiano cheese here. It is expensive, but the rich and pungent taste is really worth it.

....

1 tablespoon olive oil
1 pound Italian Turkey and Sun-Dried Tomato Sausage
  (page 22)
3 cups diced onions
2 quarts beef stock, preferably homemade (page 92)
1 cup uncooked rice (preferably arborio or California
  medium grain)

2 cups chopped fresh or canned Italian-style
  tomatoes, drained
Salt and freshly ground black pepper to taste
2 cups freshly grated Parmesan cheese
Chopped fresh parsley for garnish

....

Heat the olive oil in a heavy soup pot. Put in the sausage and cook over medium heat for 4 to 5 minutes, breaking it up as it cooks. Remove the sausage with a slotted spoon and set aside. Add the onions to the fat in the pot and cook over medium heat until totally translucent, about 10 minutes. Add the beef stock, rice, and tomatoes. Bring to a boil, reduce heat, and simmer, for 20 to 25 minutes or until the rice is tender. Return the sausage to the pot and cook for 5 minutes more. Taste for salt and pepper. Ladle the soup into bowls and sprinkle with lots of Parmesan cheese and a little parsley.

Serves 6.

Mediterranean Onion Soup

This onion soup is different from the version you might remember from Les Halles, the tumultuous, food-filled market in Paris that used to be just a hop, skip, and a stumble across the Seine from the Latin Quarter. The classic northern French *soupe à l'oignon* incorporates onions in a rich beef stock, and is usually topped with a gooey and mouth-blistering layer of bread and melted cheese. Our version originates farther south and uses our Mediterranean Sausage, vermicelli, and a lively bite of tomato along with slow-cooked onions. We suggest you serve it with crispy Homemade Garlic Croutons. The key to all well-made onion soups is to cook the onions slowly until they become light brown in color and delightfully sweet in flavor. Be patient, don't let the heat get too high and stir often so the onions caramelize evenly.

---

4 tablespoons olive oil
5 cups thinly sliced onions
Salt and freshly ground black pepper to taste
1 teaspoon sugar
1/2 pound Mediterranean Sausage (page 24)
4 cups chicken or beef stock, preferably homemade (page 92)

3 cups fresh or canned tomatoes, peeled, seeded, and puréed
    with juice
1/2 cup dried vermicelli, broken into 3- to 4-inch pieces
Homemade Garlic Croutons (following)
Chopped fresh parsley for garnish

Heat the oil in a large soup pot or Dutch oven over medium heat. Add the onions and sprinkle them with salt, pepper, and the sugar. Cover and cook, stirring from time to time, until the onions are light brown and wonderfully aromatic, 30 to 40 minutes.

Put in the sausage and fry over medium-high heat for 5 minutes, breaking it up as it cooks. Add the stock and tomatoes, and simmer for 30 minutes. Put in the vermicelli and cook until it is just al dente, 7 to 10 minutes. Taste for salt and pepper. Ladle into soup bowls and serve garnished with Homemade Garlic Croutons and chopped parsley.

Serves 6.

Homemade Garlic Croutons

Use these crisp and garlicky croutons with soups like our Mediterranean Onion Soup (page 103) and Italian Sausage Soup (page 102) or on salads such as our Italian Sausage and Spinach Salad (page 116) in place of the polenta croutons. Covered tightly, they keep in a dry, cool spot for up to 2 weeks.

1 baguette (about 25 inches) or other French or Italian bread
1/2 cup olive oil

4 cloves garlic, minced or pressed
Salt and freshly ground black pepper to taste

Preheat the oven to 375°F. Cut the bread into 1/2-inch cubes. In a large bowl, mix the olive oil with the garlic and toss the bread cubes in the flavored oil. Sprinkle cubes lightly with salt and pepper and spread out on a baking sheet. Bake until the croutons are golden brown and crisp, about 20 minutes. Cool briefly before using.

Makes 4 to 5 cups.

Middle Eastern Spinach and Meatball Soup

T his Middle Eastern favorite, known as *ash sak*, is rich with exotic flavors that are married wonderfully by the long slow cooking. It is substantial enough for a main course for lunch or light dinner, especially when served with warm pita bread and Cucumber and Yogurt Sauce (page 216).

1½ pounds Mediterranean Sausage (page 24)
2 tablespoons olive oil
2 cups chopped onions
2½ quarts water or chicken stock, preferably homemade (page 92)
2 pounds spinach, cleaned, stemmed, and chopped
1½ cups chopped Italian flat-leaf or other fresh parsley

2 teaspoons dried dill
⅔ cup uncooked medium-grain white rice
1 teaspoon ground turmeric
1 cup dried split peas
Salt and freshly ground black pepper to taste
Plain yogurt and chopped fresh or dried dill for garnish

Form 1 pound of the sausage into tiny (1-inch) meatballs. Heat the oil in a large soup pot or Dutch oven over medium heat and fry the meatballs, turning often, until all sides are browned, about 10 minutes. Remove and reserve.

Put the remaining sausage in the pot and fry for about 5 minutes, breaking it apart as it cooks. Add the onions and cook for 5 more minutes. Put in the water, spinach, parsley, dill, and rice. Cover and simmer until the rice is quite tender, about 20 minutes.

Add the turmeric and split peas and cook 30 minutes more. Return the meatballs to the pot and warm for 10 minutes. Taste for salt and pepper. Ladle into individual soup bowls and garnish with yogurt and dill.

Serves 8 to 10.

Spicy Hungarian Goulash Soup

Visitors to Hungary are often surprised when they order *gulyás* (goulash), and, instead of the expected thick stew of meat and paprika, out comes a bowl of soup. But the surprise is usually a pleasant one once they taste the rich red-brown amalgam of stock, meat, paprika, peppers, and other savory vegetables in the bowl. While it is still liquid enough to be called a soup, this dish is hearty enough to serve as a main course with a loaf of dark bread and maybe a stein or two of crisp, high-hopped German or Czech lager. Traditionally the soup would be made with mild Hungarian peppers (lighter green, longer, and narrower than our bell peppers). Bell peppers make an acceptable substitute, although if you prefer a hotter character, you might want to use Anaheim or poblano chiles. Hungarians would probably make this soup with a spicy paprika and pork sausage called *debreceni*, but our Spicy Louisiana Sausage works just as well.

---

2 tablespoons olive oil
½ pound Spicy Louisiana Sausage (page 18)
2 cups diced onions
2 cloves garlic, minced
2 tablespoons sweet Hungarian paprika
½ pound diced beef stew meat or beef chuck
2 quarts beef or chicken stock, preferably homemade
   (page 92)
1 cup tomato purée or drained diced canned tomatoes

1 teaspoon caraway seeds
1 teaspoon dried marjoram
1 bay leaf
2 cups diced unpeeled red potatoes
1 cup diced carrots
1 cup diced parsnips
2 cups diced, seeded, and deveined green bell peppers
Salt and freshly ground black pepper to taste

Heat the oil in a large, heavy soup pot or Dutch oven over medium-high heat. Fry the sausage for 5 minutes, breaking it up as it cooks. Remove the sausage with a slotted spoon and reserve, leaving all the liquids in the pot.

Put in the onions and garlic, reduce the heat to medium, and cook, stirring often, until the onions are quite soft and translucent, about 15 minutes. Stir in the paprika, and cook 1 minute to coat the vegetables well. Put in the beef and stir thoroughly for 1 minute more. Add the stock, tomato, caraway, marjoram, and bay leaf. Bring to a boil and reduce to a simmer. Partially cover and simmer for about 1 hour.

Taste a piece of the beef to make sure it is tender; if not cook a little longer. Put in the potatoes, carrots, and parsnips, and cook 15 to 20 minutes more. Add the bell peppers and the reserved sausage and cook until the peppers are quite soft, about 10 minutes. Taste for salt and pepper and serve.

Serves 6 to 8.

Chinese Two Cabbage Soup

nlike Western soups that benefit from long, slow cooking, Chinese soups are put together quickly so that the individual ingredients are fresh and eye appealing. The key is the broth—a richly flavored chicken stock with accents of ginger and green onions (recipe follows). This cabbage soup can be considered a basic recipe from which you can develop your own variations. Instead of cabbage, try watercress, Chinese greens, or spinach. You can also add diced bean curd, Chinese mushrooms, bok choy, bean sprouts, or summer squash. The essential flavor of the soup comes from the broth and seasoning along with the aromatic and spicy sausage. The vegetables and other additions can be varied depending on the season and individual tastes.

1 tablespoon peanut oil
1/2 pound Chinese Black Mushroom Sausage (page 26)
4 cups Chinese Chicken Stock (page 108)
2 cups shredded green cabbage

2 cups finely shredded napa cabbage or bok choy
Salt and freshly ground black pepper to taste
1/2 cup thinly sliced green onions, white and green parts

In a wok or large pot, heat the oil over medium-high heat. Put in the sausage and fry for 5 minutes, crumbling it as it cooks. Add the chicken stock and bring to a boil. Put in the green cabbage, reduce the heat to a simmer, and cook for 5 minutes. Add the napa cabbage and cook 1 minute more. Taste for salt and pepper. Add the green onions and ladle the soup into serving bowls. Serve at once.

Serves 4 to 6.

Chinese Chicken Stock

To make this intensely flavored chicken stock you can use a mixture of backs, feet, wings, and necks. Use leftover carcasses if you have them, but make sure that plenty of meat is still attached. It's a good idea to accumulate wing tips, necks, backs, and the like, in the freezer for later use in stock, or you can simply buy them in bulk from any butcher shop. The technique for this delicious broth is classic Chinese and was adapted from Ken Hom's book, *Fragrant Harbor Taste.*

---

3 to 4 pounds chicken backs, necks, wings, and feet
3 quarts cold water
4 slices fresh unpeeled ginger

4 whole green onions
1 teaspoon salt

Cover the chicken pieces with cold water in a large pot. Bring the liquid to a simmer. Using a skimmer or large flat spoon, remove any foam that appears on the surface. Cook the stock at a simmer, making sure that it does not come to a full boil as that would cause the stock to become cloudy and slightly bitter. Continue to skim off any foam until the stock looks fairly clear. This could take up to 30 or 40 minutes.

Add more water if necessary to make sure the chicken is covered. Put in the ginger, green onions, and salt and maintain the stock at the lowest simmer. Continue to simmer gently for 3 more hours, and from time to time, skim any fat from the surface. Strain the stock through a fine mesh strainer. Cover, refrigerate overnight, and remove any fat from the surface. Freeze some stock in tightly covered 1-quart containers for later use. Refrigerated the stock will keep for 3 to 4 days, frozen for up to 3 months.

Makes about 3 quarts.

Thai Sausage Soup

It's hard to imagine soup being popular in a climate as hot and humid as Thailand's, but spicy soups are some of the favorite dishes in this exciting cuisine and among the most delicious. Our Thai Sausage Soup is simple to make because most of the seasoning and flavor come from the sausage, which is simmered in chicken stock with vegetables and a little coconut milk. The coconut milk provides richness and a lightly sweet exotic undertone. It's available canned in most Asian groceries or by mail order (page 224), but if you can't find any, substitute condensed milk in equivalent amounts.

1 tablespoon peanut oil
1/2 pound Thai Chicken and Turkey Sausage (page 28)
1/2 cup chopped onion
1/2 cup thinly sliced celery
6 cups chicken stock (page 92) or Chinese Chicken Stock (page 108)
6 bamboo shoots,* sliced

10 medium-sized fresh mushrooms, sliced
1/2 cup coconut milk* or condensed milk
1 tablespoon fresh lime juice
Salt and freshly ground black pepper to taste
1/4 cup chopped green onions, white and green parts
Cilantro leaves for garnish
* See Glossary

Heat the oil in a large pot and stir-fry the sausage for 3 minutes over medium heat, breaking it up as it cooks. Put in the onion and celery and stir-fry for 5 more minutes. Add the chicken stock, bring to a boil, reduce the heat, and simmer for 10 minutes. Put in the bamboo shoots, mushrooms, and coconut milk. Simmer for 2 more minutes. Add the lime juice and taste for salt and pepper. Serve garnished with green onions and cilantro leaves.

Serves 6.

Senegalese Soup

We're not sure how this light and refreshing soup got its name — probably because of the hint of curry and the garnish of chopped peanuts that provide a bit of West African flavor. The soup is not particularly authentic, but it sure tastes good, either hot or cold. To cut down on fat and calories use olive oil and low-fat yogurt.

1 tablespoon butter or olive oil
1/2 pound Chicken and Apple Sausage (page 16)
1/2 cup finely chopped onion
1/2 cup finely chopped celery
1/2 cup diced, peeled, and cored green apple
2 teaspoons curry powder
1 tablespoon flour

3²/₃ cups chicken stock (page 92) or Chinese Chicken Stock (page 108)
1 cup half-and-half, light sour cream, or plain low-fat yogurt
Salt and freshly ground black peper to taste
Chopped chives and chopped salted peanuts for garnish

In a heavy 4-quart saucepan, heat the butter or oil over medium heat and sauté the sausage for 3 minutes, breaking it apart as it cooks. Put in the onion and celery and cook for 5 minutes more. Add the apple and stir in the curry powder and flour. Cook for 1 minute. Turn off the heat under the pan and stir in the chicken broth. Bring the soup to a boil over medium heat, stirring constantly, and remove from stove.

To serve the soup hot: Off the stove, stir in the half-and-half, sour cream, or yogurt. Taste for salt and pepper. Pour the soup into serving bowls and garnish with chopped chives and peanuts.

To serve the soup cold: Process the soup to a purée in a food processor or in batches in a blender. When it is cool, stir in the half-and-half, sour cream, or yogurt. Cover and chill overnight in the refrigerator. Taste for salt and pepper. Whisk to smoothness if the soup has separated. Pour into serving bowls and garnish with chopped chives and peanuts.

Serves 4 to 6.

Salads

It might seem odd to be adding sausage to salads. Fatty commercial sausage is just too greasy to eat cold, and when you add a dressing with oil the fat content might be a bit much. But with our low-fat, poultry-based sausages you can perk up your salads without these problems by adding tasty little morsels of flavor-packed poultry.

There really is no need to make up the salads beforehand since the preparation is so simple and quick. And since many of the recipes in this chapter recommend eating the salads warm or at room temperature, ingredients like rice, pasta, or lentils do not get starchy as they would after spending a night in the refrigerator. The sausage provides much of the flavor interest, and most of the salads only take a few minutes to assemble.

You can use these salads as luncheon main courses and as parts of buffets, picnics, or backyard barbecues. Some of the salads—such as our Mediterranean Seafood and Rice Salad (page 122), Marlene's Mediterranean Lentil Salad (page 120), and Italian Sausage and Spinach Salad with Polenta Croutons (page 116)—would also make great first courses for an elegant dinner party.

Chicken and Apple Sausage, Sweet Corn, and Rice Salad

ice and pasta salads are best served freshly made and warm or at room temperature. The beauty of this salad comes from its simplicity and the freshness of the ingredients. Use only the sweetest corn picked at the peak of the season. We suggest using smoked, whole milk mozzarella, usually available at good Italian delis, but you could also use smoked Gouda or another smoked cheese.

½ pound Chicken and Apple Sausage (page 16)
2 cups uncooked fresh corn kernels (scraped from cob)
2 cups freshly cooked long-grain white rice
1 cup diced smoked mozzarella or other smoked cheese

⅓ cup pine nuts, toasted (following)
1 bunch (4 to 6 ounces) watercress, leaves only
1 recipe Mustard Vinaigrette (page 121)
Salt and freshly ground black pepper to taste

Fry the sausage in a skillet over medium-high heat for 4 minutes, crumbling it as it cooks. Add the corn and cook for 3 minutes more, stirring occasionally. Placed cooked rice in a large bowl, add the hot sausage mixture and the cheese. Toss lightly to melt cheese slightly and add the toasted pine nuts and watercress leaves.

Pour the Mustard Vinaigrette over the salad in the large bowl and toss well. Taste for salt and pepper. Serve at once or at room temperature within the next 30 minutes to an hour.

Serves 4 to 6.

TO TOAST PINE NUTS

Put pine nuts in a heavy frying pan and shake continuously over medium heat until they are lightly browned and give off a toasty aroma. Transfer to a bowl and sprinkle lightly with salt. Use for other nuts (walnuts, almonds, etc.) as well.

Southwest Black Bean Salad

$\mathcal{B}$ean salads have long been a part of American picnics and buffets. This version carries on the tradition, but features the Mexican or Southwestern flavors popular today. Long a staple in Cuban cooking, black beans or turtle beans are becoming a part of mainstream American cooking for good reasons: They taste good, are quite versatile, require less cooking time than other varieties, and hold their shape well. If you don't have time to cook dry beans from scratch, drained and rinsed canned black beans work well (we recommend Progresso brand). Or you can substitute kidney beans. Just make sure that canned beans are well drained and rinsed to get rid of any "canned" taste. If using canned chiles, we prefer Ortega brand. This salad is best served warm or at room temperature. But it can also be made up a day ahead and refrigerated until serving time.

1/2 pound Southwest Green Chile Sausage (page 20) or
*   Mediterranean Sausage (page 24)*
3 cups cooked black beans (page 196) or canned black or
*   kidney beans, well rinsed and drained*
1 cup chopped red onions
2 mild green chiles,* fire-roasted (page 20), seeded, and
*   diced, or 2 canned green chiles* or 1 red bell pepper,*
*   seeded, deveined, and diced*
1 pickled jalapeño chile,* seeded and diced
1 cup chopped fresh cilantro

Garlic Lime Dressing
1 teaspoon cumin seeds
2 tablespoons fresh lime juice
1 tablespoon red wine vinegar
1 tablespoon Dijon mustard
1 teaspoon minced garlic
1/2 cup olive oil
Salt and freshly ground black pepper to taste

* See Glossary

In a skillet over medium-high heat, fry the sausage for 5 minutes, breaking it up as it cooks. Put it in a large bowl with the beans and the remaining salad ingredients.

To make the Garlic Lime Dressing: In a small heavy skillet, shake and stir the cumin seeds over medium-high heat until they begin to smoke and give off a toasty aroma. Put them in a stainless steel bowl or in a mortar, and crush them briefly with the handle of a rolling pin or a pestle. Add the lime juice, vinegar, mustard, and garlic and gradually whisk in the oil. Taste for salt and pepper.

Pour the dressing over the beans and other ingredients in the large bowl and toss well.

Serves 4 to 6.

Southwest Green Chile Sausage and Cabbage Salad

This refreshing and tangy slaw incorporates many of the flavors that make Southwestern cooking so exhilarating—chiles, citrus, and cilantro—along with crunchy carrots and cabbage. Our salad makes a wonderfully satisfying lunch, an appetizing first course, or a great side dish for our Southwest Meat Loaf (page 177). An enjoyable accompaniment is a cool glass of crisp pale ale such as Bohemia or Sierra Nevada.

2 medium carrots, diced
2 tablespoons olive oil
1 pound Southwest Green Chile Sausage (page 20)
1 head cabbage (about 1 1/2 to 2 pounds), shredded

Lime Cilantro Dressing
Juice of 6 limes
1 clove garlic, minced
1 teaspoon Tabasco
1 teaspoon salt
1/2 cup olive oil
2 bunches (4 to 6 ounces each) cilantro, chopped
Cherry tomatoes and sliced peeled oranges for garnish

In a saucepan, blanch the carrots in boiling water to cover for 5 minutes. Drain and set aside to cool. In a large skillet, panfry the sausage over medium heat in 2 tablespoons of olive oil for 4 to 5 minutes, breaking up the sausage as it browns. Combine the cooked sausage and any pan juices with the carrots and cabbage in a large bowl.

To make the Lime Cilantro Dressing: In a small bowl, whisk together the lime juice, garlic, Tabasco, salt and olive oil.

Toss the cabbage mixture with the dressing and cilantro. Place in a serving bowl and garnish with cherry tomatoes and orange slices.

Serves 6 to 8.

Italian Sausage and Spinach Salad with Polenta Croutons

We like to serve this richly flavored salad as a main course or hearty appetizer at room temperature with the spinach just barely wilted by the hot sausage. We used our Italian Turkey and Sun-Dried Tomato Sausage in this recipe, but any high quality Italian sausage can be substituted. You must use fresh basil, however. If it's out of season, just wait for summer to make the salad. That's when the tomatoes will be at their best also, and you can sit outdoors and enjoy this spicy salad in the cool of the evening with a glass or two of chilled white wine.

6 medium-sized ripe tomatoes, peeled, seeded, and diced
1/4 cup sun-dried tomatoes in olive oil
2 cups fresh basil leaves
1/3 cup fresh lemon juice
1 clove garlic, coarsely chopped
1 shallot, coarsely chopped
Salt and freshly ground black pepper to taste

3/4 cup plus 2 tablespoons extra-virgin olive oil
3/4 pound Italian Turkey with Sun-Dried Tomato Sausage (page 22)
2 bunches (16 ounces each) fresh spinach, washed and stemmed
3/4 pound fontina cheese, cut into thin strips
Polenta Croutons (following)

In a food processor or blender, mix together half the diced tomatoes with the sun-dried tomatoes, 1 cup of the basil leaves, the lemon juice, garlic, shallot, a generous pinch of salt and a little pepper. With the processor running, pour in 3/4 cup of olive oil.

Heat 2 tablespoons of olive oil in a skillet over medium heat. Fry the sausage, stirring and breaking it up as it cooks until browned and cooked through, 5 to 7 minutes.

Put the remaining diced tomatoes, the spinach, and the cheese in a large bowl, and add the fried sausages and any juices from the pan. Add the dressing and the remaining basil leaves cut into shreds. Toss well and taste for salt and pepper. Serve the salad in a shallow bowl and garnish with Polenta Croutons.

Serves 4 as a main course, 6 as a first course.

Polenta Croutons

....

If you live in a large city with a significant Italian-American population, you should be able to buy bricks of pre-made polenta at a delicatessen or specialty grocery. The blocks usually weigh one kilogram and are about two inches high and four inches wide. All you need do to make croutons is to cut quarter-inch slices from the end of the block and then cut these again into tiny strips. You can also purchase these polenta blocks by mail order (see Italian Specialty foods in Sources, page 224), or you can make up a batch of polenta from scratch. In any case, you will have some leftover polenta, which can be sliced and fried and served with a spicy tomato sauce for a delightful snack or side dish. Our Homemade Garlic Croutons (page 104) may be substituted, as can store-bought bread croutons, but the results won't be as delicious.

Cooked polenta (either purchased in a block or $1/2$ recipe homemade, page 161)
$1/3$ cup finely ground yellow cornmeal
$1/2$ cup corn oil
$1/4$ cup freshly grated Parmesan cheese

If using a precooked polenta block, cut eight 2 x 4 x $1/4$-inch slices from the block, and cut each slice into 2 x $1/4$ x $1/4$-inch strips (you should end up with approximately 128 strips). If you are making polenta from scratch, as soon as it is cooked, spread the polenta on a cookie sheet to form an even $1/4$-inch layer. When cooled and set, cut the polenta into 2 x $1/4$ x $1/4$-inch strips. In a large bowl, toss the polenta strips with the cornmeal until lightly coated.

Heat the corn oil in a 10-inch skillet over medium-high heat. Fry the polenta sticks in batches (do not crowd), turning frequently, until lightly browned, about 7 minutes. Drain briefly on paper towels, and toss with Parmesan cheese. Serve *immediately*. The croutons do not store well, but leftover polenta can be kept covered in the refrigerator for up to 2 weeks.

Makes about 6 dozen strips.

Spaghettini and Crispy Sausage Salad

The best pasta salads are simple and freshly made. In this version, sweet ripe tomatoes are barely cooked and then tossed with warm spaghettini. What makes this pasta salad extra special are crispy bites of sausage that contrast beautifully with the pasta and tomato. For the bread crumbs, we prefer to use the Japanese brand of bread crumbs, Panko (see Glossary), or to make bread crumbs at home from two-day-old Italian or French bread in a food processor or blender. Use store-bought bread crumbs only as a last resort as they are generally too fine and often have a stale cardboard taste.

---

1 pound dried spaghettini or thin spaghetti
4 tablespoons olive oil
1 clove garlic, chopped
4 ripe tomatoes, diced
Vegetable oil for deep frying
½ pound Italian Turkey Sausage with Sun-Dried Tomatoes (page 22), Mediterranean Sausage (page 24), or good quality Italian sausage
1 egg, lightly beaten

1 cup milk
2 cups Japanese Panko or homemade bread crumbs
1 tablespoon drained capers
½ cup pitted and chopped Italian or Greek black olives
1 tablespoon red wine vinegar
¼ cup shredded fresh basil (if unavailable, use chives or green onions; do not use dried basil)
Salt and freshly ground black pepper to taste

Cook spaghettini in a large pot of lightly salted boiling water until al dente, about 8 to 9 minutes. Drain, and toss with 2 tablespoons of the olive oil. Reserve.

Heat the remaining olive oil in a small nonreactive saucepan over medium heat. Add the garlic and cook for 1 minute. Add the tomatoes, cook 2 minutes more, stirring occasionally. Remove from heat and reserve.

In a heavy saucepan or Dutch oven large enough to hold 3 to 4 inches of oil with plenty of extra space, heat the vegetable oil for deep-frying to 375°F. (If you don't have a thermometer, test oil by dropping in a few bread crumbs. They should begin browning immediately.) Form the sausage into 1-inch meatballs.

In a small bowl, mix together the egg and milk. Dip each meatball in the egg and milk mixture and then fully coat with the bread crumbs. Deep-fry meatballs in batches of 8 to 10 each until lightly browned, 3 to 4 minutes per batch. Drain on paper towels.

Quickly assemble the salad in a large serving bowl by tossing the pasta with the garlic-tomato mixture along with the crispy sausage bites. Add the remaining ingredients. Taste for salt and pepper. Serve at once.

Serves 4 to 6.

Mediterranean Orzo Salad

Orzo, a tiny rice-shaped pasta, is combined with our Mediterranean Sausage, pine nuts, feta, and olives in this tangy salad. As with most pasta salads, it is best served fresh at room temperature, but it can be refrigerated for later use. In Greece, North Africa, and all around the Mediterranean, ricelike pastas or grains such as orzo, couscous, and pastina are used in soups, stews, and salads. These small pastas absorb flavors wonderfully and provide a chewy texture in salads and soups. This flavorful salad makes a dramatic center-piece for an alfresco lunch with a glass or two of light Italian white wine such as Gavi or Galestro.

Lemon and Garlic Dressing
1/4 cup fresh lemon juice
1 tablespoon grated lemon zest
1 tablespoon Dijon mustard
1 teaspoon minced garlic
1 tablespoon dried Greek oregano
3/4 cup extra-virgin olive oil
Salt and freshly ground black pepper to taste

For the Salad
1 pound Mediterranean Sausage (page 24)
2 cups cooked orzo or other rice-shaped pasta (orzo triples when cooked)
1/3 cup pistachio or pine nuts, toasted (page 113)
6 green onions, white and green parts, thinly sliced
1/4 pound feta cheese
10 Kalamata olives, pitted and coarsely chopped
1 bunch watercress, leaves only, chopped

Whisk together the dressing ingredients or shake well in a closed jar. Taste for salt and pepper.

In a large skillet, fry the sausage over medium heat for 4 to 5 minutes, breaking it up as it cooks. In a large bowl, toss the cooked sausage with all the remaining ingredients except the watercress. Toss with the dressing; taste for salt and pepper.

Arrange the salad in a shallow bowl or platter and sprinkle on the chopped watercress.

Serves 4 to 6.

Marlene's Mediterranean Lentil Salad

I f you can find them, the tiny green French lentils work best for this tangy salad. They cook up quickly, hold their shape, and seem to have more flavor than other varieties. Otherwise, use ordinary brown lentils, but take care not to overcook them. The lentils should be tender, but still hold their shape. We use Laura Chenel's excellent fresh chèvre in this recipe, but any fresh goat cheese would do well. To keep the walnuts crisp and crunchy, add them at the last minute, just before serving. Marlene Levinson, a San Francisco cooking teacher and creator of innovative salads, serves this flavorful and substantial salad with a cold poached vegetable such as green beans or broccoli for a light, but satisfying lunch. Being a frugal cook, she recommends saving the cooking liquid from the lentils as a basis for a lentil or bean soup.

---

2 cups dried French or other lentils
4 cups chicken stock
2 bay leaves
1/2 teaspoon dried thyme
4 tablespoons olive oil
1/2 pound Mediterranean Sausage (page 24) or Italian

Turkey and Sun-Dried Tomato Sausage (page 22)
1/2 cup chopped fresh parsley
4 ounces fresh goat cheese
1 cup shelled walnut halves
Mustard Vinaigrette (following)
Salt and freshly ground black pepper to taste

Pick over the lentils for rocks or other debris and rinse with cold water. Bring the stock to a boil in a large pot and add the lentils, bay leaves, and thyme. Lower the heat and cook until the lentils are just tender, about 15 minutes. If they need more cooking, sample a lentil every few minutes to make sure they don't overcook. Drain the lentils and save the stock for soup. Cool the lentils under running water, drain, and put in a mixing bowl.

In a skillet, fry the sausage in 2 tablespoons of the oil for 5 minutes, breaking it up as it cooks. Add all but about 4 tablespoons of the sausage to the lentils, along with any juices in the skillet. Put in the parsley. Dice the cheese and add it to the lentils, reserving a few tablespoons for garnish. In a small pan over low heat, fry the walnuts in the remaining 2 tablespoons of oil until they are lightly brown and smell nutty. Add the nuts and any oil in the pan to the lentils.

Pour the dressing over the lentils and mix the salad until it is well blended. Taste for salt and pepper. Spoon the salad into a shallow bowl or platter and garnish with remaining bits of sausage and cheese. Serve warm or at room temperature.

Serves 6.

Mustard Vinaigrette

Not only good on lentils, this mustardy dressing is also delicious on cold poached fish or seafood.

1 tablespoon Dijon mustard
2 tablespoons red wine vinegar

½ cup extra-virgin olive oil
Salt and freshly ground black pepper to taste

To make the vinaigrette, whisk together the mustard and vinegar in a small bowl, and then gradually beat in the oil. Taste for salt and pepper.

Makes about ¾ cup.

Mediterranean Seafood and Rice Salad

One reason we love rice so much is that it absorbs flavors so well. Some of our favorite rice dishes are jambalaya, paella, and risotto—all good examples of how rich flavors can permeate rice. Cheap and filling, rice is a staple for a good part of the world's population. But in India, basmati rice with its unique nutty taste and aroma is reserved for festive occasions. Once hard to find, imported basmati and its American-grown cousin Texmati are now stocked at many supermarkets. If you can't find it, use any good quality long-grain white rice or order by direct mail (see Sources, page 224). Here basmati is combined in a salad with seafood and a flavorful sausage for a wonderful lunch or first course. Rock shrimp and squid are not expensive as seafood goes and work well here. If mussels are in season, a dozen or two can also be cooked and added to the salad. We adapted this tasty seafood salad from a recipe by Nancy Oakes, Bruce's wife and owner/chef of Boulevard restaurant in San Francisco. *San Francisco Focus* voted her Chef of the Year in 1993 and *Food and Wine* magazine named her one of America's ten best chefs in the same year.

TO CLEAN SQUID

Separate the body from the head and tentacles and cut the tentacles just below the eyes. Discard heads, reserve tentacles. Remove the beak from tentacles and discard. Pull film and fins from outside body. Remove quill and any milky film from inside body. Wash the body sack thoroughly inside and out under cold running water. Body may be left whole or cut into rings or strips. Tentacles are used whole.

Rice

1 tablespoon olive oil
1/2 pound Mediterranean Sausage (page 24)
1 cup basmati, Texmati, or long-grain white rice
1 cup chopped onion
2 cloves garlic, chopped
1 cup ripe tomatoes, peeled, seeded, and diced
2 cups chicken stock, preferably homemade (page 92)
1/2 teaspoon salt
1/4 teaspoon freshly ground black pepper

Seafood

2 tablespoons olive oil
1/2 pound raw rock shrimp or other medium-sized shrimp,
peeled and deveined
1/2 pound squid, cleaned (page 122), and sliced into rounds
2 cloves garlic, chopped
2 green onions, white and green parts, thinly sliced
1 dozen mussels (optional), scrubbed with beards removed
2 cups diced, peeled, and deveined red bell pepper
1/2 teaspoon red pepper flakes
1 cup chopped fresh cilantro

Dressing

Juice of 1 lemon
1 tablespoon sherry vinegar
1/4 cup olive oil
Salt and freshly ground black pepper to taste

To make the rice: In a heavy saucepan or deep skillet, heat the oil over medium-high heat and brown the sausage for 3 minutes, breaking it apart as it cooks. Add the rice and cook, stirring constantly, for 3 minutes more. Stir in the onions and garlic, and cook until the onions are soft, about 5 minutes more. Put in the tomatoes, stir, and cook 1 minute. Add the stock, salt, and pepper. Bring to a boil, reduce heat to low, and cover. Simmer for 15 minutes. Allow the rice to stand in the covered pot for 5 minutes off the heat. Fluff the rice with a fork and reserve.

To make the seafood: In a skillet, heat the oil over medium-high heat and stir in the shrimp. Cook for 1 minute. Stir in the squid, garlic, and green onions, and cook 1 minute more until the shrimp is pink and firm. Remove seafood from the pan with a slotted spoon and add the mussels, if using, stirring and tossing them in the pan as they cook. As the mussels open, remove them from the pan. Add the bell pepper and red pepper flakes to the pan, and cook for 2 to 3 minutes. Mix the peppers with the seafood and stir in the chopped cilantro. Discard any mussels that do not open. Set seafood aside.

To make the dressing: In a small bowl, whisk together the lemon and vinegar. Add the olive oil in a steady stream while continuing to whisk. Taste for salt and pepper.

To assemble the salad: In a large bowl, mix together the rice, seafood, and dressing and spoon onto a large platter. Arrange the mussels, if using, around the edge.

Serves 4 generously as a lunch, 6 to 8 as a first course.

Thai Sausage Salad

Thai food is characterized by lively flavors, very little fat, and substantial heat levels from pepper and chiles. These appealing qualities are most clearly shown in the many salads found on Thai tables. Cold salads of squid or shrimp or grilled beef, pork, or chicken are found all over Thailand and in many Thai restaurants in America. The chewy seafood or meat is contrasted with crisp ingredients like red onions and lettuce with all the flavors tied together by tangy limes and hot chiles. Thai salads make delightful first courses and can also serve as main dishes when paired with Thai Fried Rice (page 198) or preceded by a spicy soup (see Thai Sausage Soup, page 109).

---

*1 pound Thai Chicken and Turkey Sausage (page 28),
    formed into 2-inch patties, 1/2 inch thick*
1/3 cup fresh lime juice
2 to 3 teaspoons Sriracha Thai sweet chili sauce or
    Tabasco*
Pinch sugar
2 tablespoons soy sauce

20 fresh mint leaves
1 tablespoon thinly sliced lemongrass* (center stalks only)
1/2 red onion, thinly sliced
*1 medium head iceberg lettuce, large outer leaves removed
    and kept whole, remaining leaves thinly sliced*
Cilantro sprigs for garnish

* See Glossary

In a large nonstick skillet, panfry the sausage patties over medium heat, until lightly browned and cooked through, 5 to 7 minutes. Set aside sausage and reserve pan drippings.

In a small bowl, combine drippings from the sausage pan with the lime juice, chili sauce, sugar, and soy sauce. Add the mint leaves, lemongrass, and sliced onion to this dressing and stir well.

Lay the large lettuce leaves on a platter and cover with the shredded lettuce. Arrange the sausage patties over the lettuce. Spoon the dressing all over the salad, and garnish with cilantro sprigs.

Serves 4 to 6.

Chinese Salad with Ginger Orange Dressing

*I*n many Chinese dishes, texture and mouth feel are often as important as taste. This salad combines crisp cabbage and cucumbers, crunchy peanuts and bean sprouts along with silky-textured black mushrooms and a lively bite of onion and cilantro. These flavors and textures are brought together by a sweet and tangy dressing that mixes garlic and chili oil together with orange juice and ginger. We are sure this flavorful salad will become an instant favorite, whether served warm or cold. It is particularly refreshing on hot summer nights with a glass of cold dry Gewurztraminer from Alsace or from California's Mendocino County.

1 pound Chinese Black Mushroom Sausage (page 26)
1 tablespoon peanut or other vegetable oil
6 green onions, white and green parts, cut into 1-inch pieces
1 cup chopped red onion
1 cucumber, peeled, seeded, and cut into matchstick-sized pieces

1 1/2 cups fresh bean sprouts
3 cups finely shredded napa cabbage or white cabbage
1 recipe Ginger Orange Dressing (following)
Salt and freshly ground black pepper to taste
1/2 cup dry roasted peanuts
1/4 cup chopped fresh cilantro

Form the sausage into 1/2 inch bits. Fry in the peanut oil over medium-high heat in a 12-inch skillet for 5 minutes, shaking the pan and stirring to brown the bits on all sides. Stir in the green onions and red onion, and cook for 1 minute more. Remove from heat and mix with the cucumber, bean sprouts, and cabbage in a large bowl.

Pour the dressing over the vegetables and sausage mixture in the large bowl. Toss well. Taste for salt and pepper. Garnish with the peanuts and cilantro.

Serves 4 to 6.

Ginger Orange Dressing

Shredded raw cabbage tossed with this tangy dressing makes a great condiment for a sandwich (page 62). The dressing is also wonderful over lightly steamed asparagus or broccoli, and creates a great first course when poured over chilled cooked prawns, lobster tails, and/or scallops.

1 clove minced garlic
1 tablespoon minced fresh ginger
1 teaspoon sugar
2 tablespoons sherry vinegar or rice vinegar
*1 teaspoon Asian chili oil**

*1 tablespoon Asian sesame oil**
1/4 cup fresh orange juice
2 tablespoons soy sauce
*2 tablespoons Asian peanut oil**

* See Glossary

In a small bowl, whisk together all the dressing ingredients.

Makes about 3/4 cup.

"Minced Squab" in Lettuce Cups

A classic Chinese banquet dish is made from meat painstakingly removed from squab carcasses and then minced and flavored, making it a preparation that is both tedious and expensive. By replacing the squab with our Chinese Black Mushroom Sausage, we've simplified the dish considerably, without any loss of flavor or elegance. Many of the flavors usually mixed with the squab such as ginger, garlic, and black mushrooms are already in the sausage, and thus it is a simple task to put everything together. We've included this recipe in our salad section because of the lettuce leaves in which the squab is traditionally rolled, but the dish is best served as a starter course for a Chinese banquet or as a lovely meal when paired with our Thai Fried Rice (page 198) or Edy's Chinese Stuffed Fish (page 152) with steamed rice.

2 tablespoons peanut oil
1 pound Chinese Black Mushroom Sausage (page 26)
1 clove garlic, minced
8 canned water chestnuts,* finely chopped
¾ cup finely chopped bamboo shoots*
2 green onions, white and green parts, finely chopped
⅓ cup chicken stock
2 tablespoons sherry

1 teaspoon sugar
1 tablespoon soy sauce
1 tablespoon oyster sauce*
1 teaspoon cornstarch dissolved in 1 tablespoon water
8 to 12 iceberg or bibb lettuce leaves, trimmed to 6- to 7-inch rounds

*See Glossary

As with most Chinese recipes, it's best to have all the ingredients premeasured, chopped, and ready to use. Heat a large wok or heavy skillet over high heat. Add the oil and heat for 30 seconds until it just begins to smoke. Add the sausage and garlic, and stir-fry, turning and chopping the mixture continuously as it cooks, for 2 minutes. Put in the water chestnuts and bamboo shoots, and stir-fry for 1 minute more. Add the green onions, chicken stock, sherry, sugar, soy sauce, and oyster sauce. Cook over high heat, stirring often, until the liquid has almost been absorbed. Stir the cornstarch mixture and rapidly stir it into the wok. Cook until thickened, about 30 seconds.

Transfer the mixture to a platter or shallow bowl and bring it to the table with the lettuce leaves arranged on another platter. Guests serve themselves by placing 2 to 3 tablespoons of the mixture in the center of a lettuce leaf, folding the leaf over, and then rolling it into a cylinder. This dish is best eaten by hand, but you can attempt to eat it with chopsticks as the Chinese do.

Serves 6 to 8 as part of a large banquet or 4 as a first course.

Pasta

asta is one of the most versatile foods available today, and it has the added advantage of being easy to prepare and inexpensive. Using our low-fat poultry sausages, you can make a great range of delicious pasta dishes quickly and with a minimum of calories.

We've adapted some of the best traditonal Italian dishes using our Italian Turkey and Sun-Dried Tomato Sausage, pairing this spicy and healthy sausage with many varieties and shapes of pasta. Capellini with Sausage, Lemon, and Basil (page 133), Baked Penne with Sausage, Sun-Dried Tomatoes, and Ricotta (page 134), and Spaghettini with Sausage, Anchovies, and Bread Crumbs (page 139) are all Italian-inspired dishes that make flavorful first courses, luncheon dishes, or light main courses.

Pasta combines wonderfully with vegetables and sausage in our Broccoli Rabe and Sausage with Rotellini and Balsamic Vinegar (page 143), Penne with Roasted Tomatoes and Eggplant (page 141), and Linguine with Italian Sausage and Arugula (page 137). We've also lightened up some old Italian-American favorites in our Spaghetti with Sausage and Fresh Tomato Sauce (page 136) and Cheese and Sausage Ravioli with Fresh Tomato and Basil Sauce (page 144).

And don't forget, pasta originated in Asia. Savory noodles are still one of the most popular staples in Southeast Asia, China, and Japan. Our Thai Noodle Stir-Fry (page 131) and Singapore Noodles with Black Mushroom Sausage (page 132) provide the flavors of the East in these light and flavorful pasta dishes.

Tips for Cooking Pasta

Cooking pasta is easy and quick, but for best results try the following tips:

• Use a big pot that doesn't crowd the noodles, and plenty of water. Bring the water to a rolling boil, add a generous pinch or two of salt, and put in the pasta all at once.

• Stir the pasta well (one of those special pasta forks is helpful) to make sure the pasta doesn't clump together or stick to the bottom of the pot.

• Time of cooking is important—don't believe everything you read, on the packages or even in our recipes. Cooking times vary widely, depending on the size and relative dryness of the pasta. Generally, fresh pasta cooks fastest, thin pasta faster than thick, straight pasta is done sooner than the bent or twisted or stuffed varieties. Use the cooking times as a rough guide, but be sure to pull out a strand or two after a few minutes and taste. Al dente means that the pasta is still a bit resistant "to the tooth."

• Drain pasta well before adding sauce. Some cooks like to wash cooked pasta under cold running water and then reheat in the sauce. If you're going to keep drained pasta for more than a couple of minutes, toss it in some olive oil so it won't stick together.

Thai Noodle Stir-Fry

These sweet and sour noodles are called *pad Thai* in Thai restaurants, and some version or other of this dish is found on every Thai menu we've ever seen. Our recipe is adapted from *Real Thai* by Nancie McDermott and uses our Thai Chicken and Turkey Sausage instead of the more usual shrimp. Quick, simple, light, and delicious, these noodles should prove very popular with family and friends, especially when paired with Thai Sausage Satay (page 45) and Nancy's Asian Dipping Sauce (page 48).

....

1 pound dried rice stick noodles*
3 tablespoons peanut oil
2 tablespoons sliced garlic
2 teaspoons chopped fresh ginger
1/2 pound Thai Chicken and Turkey Sausage (page 28)
2 eggs, beaten
1/4 cup Southeast Asian fish sauce*
1 tablespoon light soy sauce

1 tablespoon sugar
2 tablespoons catsup
1/3 cup chopped dry-roasted peanuts
4 cups bean sprouts
10 green onions, white and green parts, cut into 2-inch lengths
2 limes, cut into wedges
* See Glossary

....

Cover the rice stick noodles with warm water and soak until very limp and white, at least 20 minutes. Drain and set aside.

Heat 1 tablespoon of the oil in a large wok or heavy nonstick skillet over medium-high heat. Put in the garlic and ginger and stir-fry for 30 seconds, taking care not to burn the garlic. Add the sausage and stir-fry for 3 minutes, breaking the sausage up as it cooks. Remove from the pan to a bowl.

Add 1 tablespoon of the oil to the wok and pour in the eggs. Tilt the pan to spread the eggs out evenly to form a thin omelet. As soon as they begin to set, stir-fry to scramble the eggs coarsely. Add the eggs to the sausage mixture.

Heat the last tablespoon of the oil in the wok over high heat and add the soaked, drained noodles. Using a spatula, spread the noodles into a thin cake and then fold them back into a clump. Repeat this process until the noodles soften and curl, about 3 minutes. Stir in the fish sauce, soy sauce, sugar, catsup, and peanuts. Toss for 30 seconds to coat noodles.

Put 3 cups of the bean sprouts and the green onions in the wok, and add the sausage and egg mixture. Stir-fry and toss for 1 minute over high heat. Transfer the noodles to a shallow bowl or platter and garnish with the remaining bean sprouts and the wedges of lime.

Serves 4.

Singapore Noodles with Black Mushroom Sausage

3 tablespoons peanut oil
1 egg, lightly beaten
1 pound fresh Chinese vermicelli noodles*
1/2 pound Chinese Black Mushroom Sausage (page 26)
1 tablespoon chopped garlic
1/4 pound small shrimp, peeled and deveined
3 tablespoons Chinese fermented black beans*, chopped
1 teaspoon red pepper flakes

2 tablespoons sherry
1 tablespoon Asian sesame oil*
1/2 cup chicken stock (page 92), or Chinese Chicken Stock (page 108)
2 cups thinly sliced napa cabbage, bok choy, or green cabbage
6 green onions, white and green parts, chopped

* See Glossary

In a small, nonstick skillet, heat 1 or 2 teaspoons of the oil over medium-high heat. Add the egg and spread it out evenly to form a very thin omelet. Cook just until the egg has set, 30 seconds to a minute, then turn over carefully and cook for 30 seconds more. Transfer the omelet to a plate, cool, roll it up, and then cut it crosswise into thin strips. Reserve.

Add the noodles to a large pot of lightly salted water. Cook for 1 to 2 minutes, drain, and then toss the noodles with a bit of oil to prevent clumping. Set aside and keep warm while you prepare the rest of the dish.

Add the remaining peanut oil to a wok or large skillet over high heat. Put in the sausage and stir-fry for 1 minute, breaking it up as it cooks. Add the garlic, shrimp, black beans, red pepper flakes, sherry, and sesame oil. Stir-fry for 1 more minute. Pour in the chicken stock and bring to a boil. Add the cabbage and stir-fry until it wilts, 2 to 3 minutes.

Arrange the cooked noodles on a platter or shallow bowl. Put the sausage-cabbage mixture over the noodles and top with the reserved egg strips and the green onions. Just before serving, toss the noodles with the sausage, cabbage, and garnishes. The noodles are equally good hot or at room temperature.

Serves 4 to 6.

Capellini with Sausage, Lemon, and Basil

DENIS SAYS:

"I ENJOYED A LEMONY PASTA LIKE THIS ONE BRIGHT SPRING AFTERNOON ON A TERRACE NEAR TRENTO IN THE FOOTHILLS OF THE ALPS. A GLASS OF FRESH, CRISP PINOT BIANCO FROM THE VINEYARDS ON THE HILLS ABOVE PICKED UP THE LIGHT CITRUS FLAVORS AND FRESH HERBS IN THE PASTA WITH THE FRUITY OLIVE OIL AND EARTHY SAUSAGE, PROVIDING BASS NOTES. SOMETIMES YOU WONDER WHAT ALL THOSE ITALIAN ANGELS ARE SINGING ABOUT IN THE PAINTINGS—AND THEN SUDDENLY YOU KNOW!"

1 pound dried capellini or other thin pasta
1 tablespoon extra-virgin olive oil
½ pound Italian Turkey and Sun-Dried Tomato Sausage (page 22) or other good quality Italian sausage
Zest of 2 lemons, cut into fine julienne strips

5 tablespoons fresh lemon juice
20 fresh basil leaves, shredded
5 tablespoons minced fresh parsley
Salt and freshly ground black pepper to taste
Freshly grated Parmesan cheese (optional)

Cook the capellini in a large pot of salted boiling water to the al dente stage, about 5 to 6 minutes, and drain. Meanwhile, in a large skillet sauté the sausage in the olive oil over medium heat for 4 to 6 minutes, breaking it up as it cooks. Add the lemon zest, lemon juice, basil, and parsley. Cook 1 minute more. When the pasta is done, drain and toss with the sausage mixture until well coated. Season with salt and pepper and, if you like, sprinkle with Parmesan.

Serves 4 to 6.

Baked Penne with Sausage, Sun-Dried Tomatoes, and Ricotta

This simple baked pasta has the flavor and character of lasagna without all the work and with a lot less fat. You can make it up the night before a party or special dinner, refrigerate it, and bake it the next day. This recipe can be varied easily. You can mix in a half cup of a fresh goat cheese such as Laura Chenel's. Or to give this dish a Middle Eastern note, use our Mediterranean Sausage (page 24), mix a half cup of feta cheese with the ricotta, and substitute fresh or dried Greek oregano for the basil.

1 pound dried penne or other tubular pasta
2 tablespoons extra-virgin olive oil
³/₄ pound Italian Turkey and Sun-Dried Tomato Sausage
   (page 22)
2 to 3 cups coarsely chopped spinach

¹/₂ pound fresh tomatoes, coarsely chopped
¹/₂ pound low-fat ricotta cheese
10 fresh basil leaves, sliced into 1/4-inch ribbons
Salt and freshly ground black pepper to taste

Preheat the oven to 350°F. Cook the penne in a large pot of salted boiling water until al dente, about 10 minutes, and drain. Meanwhile, heat the olive oil in a large skillet and sauté the sausage over medium-high heat for 4 to 5 minutes, breaking it up as it cooks. Put in the spinach and cook until wilted.

In a large mixing bowl, mix together the sausage and spinach with the tomatoes, ricotta, and basil. Add the cooked, drained penne to the other ingredients in the bowl and mix well. Taste for salt and pepper. Place the pasta mixture in a shallow greased 9x13-inch baking dish and bake until the cheese is bubbly, about 20 minutes.

Serves 4 to 6.

Pasta with Sausage and Beans

This hearty dish is based on one of Italy's most famous and nutritious soup/stews, *pasta e fagioli*, also known as *pasta fa'zool*. Mixing pasta with beans (*fagioli*) does sound a bit starchy, but this simple peasant dish has plenty of flavor from the sausage and vegetables, and is a good choice for a fall football party or a New Year's Day buffet with our Italian Sausage and Spinach Salad with Polenta Croutons (page 116). Our version is easy to make, and combines precooked white beans (preferably cannellini beans) with orecchiette or other large twisted pasta. You can cook the beans yourself (see Lalime's Black Beans, page 196) or use some of the excellent canned Italian-style cannellini beans (Progresso brand is quite good).

1/2 pound dried orecchiette, bow-ties (farfalle), pin wheels, or other large twisted pasta
3 tablespoons olive oil
1/2 pound Italian Turkey and Sun-Dried Tomato Sausage (page 22) or other good quality Italian sausage
1 cup chopped onion
1 cup chopped carrot

2 cups chopped, peeled, and seeded fresh tomatoes or drained and chopped canned Italian-style tomatoes
2 cups cooked white beans (cannellini, Great Northern, or navy beans)
2 fresh sage leaves or 1/2 teaspoon dried sage
Salt and freshly ground black pepper to taste
1/2 cup freshly grated Parmesan cheese

Cook the pasta in a large pot of salted boiling water to the al dente stage, as directed on the package, and drain. While the pasta is cooking, prepare the sauce.

In a large deep skillet, heat 2 tablespoons of the olive oil over medium-high heat. Add the sausage and cook for 3 minutes, breaking it up as it cooks. Put in the onions and carrots and cook until the onions are translucent, about 5 minutes, stirring often. Add the tomatoes, cooked beans, and sage, cover, and cook until the carrots are just tender, about 10 minutes.

Mix in the pasta and taste for salt and pepper. Transfer to a shallow serving bowl, and drizzle with the remaining tablespoon of olive oil. Serve in shallow bowls, garnished with Parmesan cheese.

Serves 4.

Spaghetti with Sausage and Fresh Tomato Sauce

This basic recipe can be embellished with diced roasted eggplant, zucchini, peas, or other cooked vegetables such as broccoli, cauliflower, asparagus, or green beans. You could even add diced leftover chicken for extra richness. For a bit of crunchiness and added flavor, garnish the pasta with toasted nuts such as pine nuts, walnuts, or pecans (see page 113). Other sausages that would do well here are our Mediterranean Sausage (page 24) and Spicy Louisiana Sausage (page 18).

1 pound dried spaghetti or other long pasta (such as linguine or fettuccine)

1 tablespoon olive oil

1 pound Italian Turkey and Sun-Dried Tomato Sausage (page 22) or other good quality Italian sausage

³/₄ cup white wine

2 tablespoons tomato paste

2 ripe tomatoes, diced

25 basil leaves, chopped

Cook the spaghetti in a large pot of salted boiling water until al dente, about 8 to 9 minutes, and drain. Meanwhile, heat the olive oil in a skillet over medium heat. Add the sausage and brown for 4 to 5 minutes, crumbling it as it cooks. Put in the wine and tomato paste, stir well, and cook for 5 minutes more. Add the diced tomatoes and cook for 2 minutes more. (At this point you could add cooked vegetables, diced chicken, nuts, etc.) Add the chopped basil and toss the drained cooked pasta with the sauce. Transfer to a platter and serve.

Serves 4 to 6.

Linguine with Italian Sausage and Arugula

This is a wonderful dish for summer dining. It only takes minutes to prepare, and is just as good at room temperature as when served hot from the pan. You can cook this light and spicy pasta quickly in the kitchen and serve it later on the deck or patio in the cool of the evening. You might want to accompany it with a glass of chilled Pinot Grigio, some Italian bread, and a salad of romaine leaves dressed in extra virgin olive oil and balsamic vinegar. Arugula has a unique bitter and nutty flavor that marries well with sausage. If you can't find it, you could substitute watercress, chard leaves, or spinach.

1 pound dried linguine or spaghetti
2 tablespoons olive oil
1/2 pound Italian Turkey and Sun-Dried Tomato Sausage
  (page 22)

4 cloves garlic, sliced thinly
1/2 teaspoon red pepper flakes
1 pound arugula, washed and dried
Freshly grated Parmesan cheese

Cook the linguine in a large pot of salted boiling water until al dente, about 9 to 10 minutes, and drain. Meanwhile, heat the oil in a large skillet over medium heat and sauté the sausage for 5 minutes, breaking it apart as it cooks. Add the garlic and red pepper flakes and fry for about 30 seconds, stirring well. Put in the arugula and cook over medium heat until it begins to wilt. Simmer for 2 minutes, adding small amounts of water if the pan seems too dry. Toss the sausage and arugula mixture with the drained, cooked pasta and sprinkle with grated Parmesan cheese.

Serves 4 to 6.

Rigatoni with Sausage and Yogurt Sauce

One of the tastiest and simplest ways to use sausage with pasta is to simmer fried crumbled sausage with cream. Sometimes a bit of tomato paste or cheese can be added, and that's all there is to it. The creamy sauce is really delicious, but it is pretty heavy on the calories. So to lighten the dish a bit and still keep the rich flavors, we've replaced the cream with yogurt. It works just as well, giving the sauce a creamy texture without all the fat, while providing a tart undertone that wakes up the taste buds. But be careful when using yogurt, as it curdles easily; let the sauce cool a bit before you add the yogurt off the heat. It's better to serve this dish warm and not piping hot, rather than risk the yogurt curdling. Mediterranean Sausage (page 24) or Southwest Green Chile Sausage (page 20) can be used here for different, but just as enjoyable, flavors.

¼ cup chopped sun-dried tomatoes, dry or packed in oil*
1 pound dried rigatoni or other tubular pasta (such as ziti or penne)
1 tablespoon olive oil
1 pound Italian Turkey and Sun-Dried Tomato Sausage

(page 22) or other high quality Italian sausage
½ cup low-fat or nonfat plain yogurt
¼ cup freshly grated Parmesan cheese

*See Glossary

If using dry-packed tomatoes, soak them in boiling water to cover for ½ hour before chopping. Take sun-dried tomatoes packed in oil right out of the jar and chop. Cook the rigatoni in a large pot of salted boiling water until al dente, about 11 to 12 minutes, and drain. Meanwhile, heat the olive oil in a large skillet and fry the sausage for 4 to 5 minutes over medium-high heat, breaking it up as it browns. Add the sun-dried tomatoes and cook for 2 more minutes, stirring well. Remove the skillet from the heat, cool for 2 minutes, and stir in the yogurt. Toss with the cooked, drained pasta and the grated cheese.

Serves 4 to 6.

Spaghettini with Sausage, Anchovies, and Bread Crumbs

In southern Italy, cooking is based on pasta served with inexpensive, but highly flavored ingredients such as olives, anchovies, garlic, and garden vegetables. Very little meat and cheese are used on the everyday table. When meat does find its way into the cuisine, it is often sausage used sparingly, more as a flavoring or condiment than as a main ingredient. Instead of garnishing the pasta with expensive cheese, crunchy toasted bread crumbs are often strewn over the pasta just before serving. Southern Italian cooking satisfies concerns for low-fat food and packs plenty of flavor into each bite. It has the added benefit of being inexpensive when compared to the richer northern dishes using meat and cheese. Use any high quality thin dried pasta such as spaghetti, vermicelli, spaghettini, tagliarini, or capellini for this piquant dish.

1 tablespoon olive oil
1/2 pound Italian Turkey and Sun-Dried Tomato Sausage
    (page 22) or other good quality Italian sausage
3/4 pound spaghettini or other thin dried pasta
6 anchovy fillets, washed and finely chopped

Pinch red pepper flakes
1/4 cup chopped fresh Italian flat-leaf parsley or
    regular parsley
1 recipe Toasted Bread Crumbs (following)

Heat the olive oil in a skillet over medium-high heat. Put in the sausage and cook for 5 minutes, breaking it up as it cooks. Remove pan from heat and reserve.

Meanwhile, boil 3 to 4 quarts of lightly salted water in a large pot, add the pasta, and cook until almost done (as directed on package). Put the pan with the sausage back on the stove over medium heat and add the anchovy and red pepper flakes. Cook 1 minute, stirring well. Add 3 to 4 tablespoons of the pasta water to the pan and stir well. Drain the pasta and toss with the sauce. Transfer to a shallow bowl and sprinkle with the parsley and bread crumbs. Serve at once.

Serves 4.

Toasted Bread Crumbs

....

In this recipe the toasted crumbs are made by frying day-old Italian or French bread crumbs in olive oil; they are much like mini croutons, and can be used on pasta and in salads equally well. You can add more flavor by briefly frying a clove of garlic or two in the oil and removing before toasting crumbs and/or tossing the fried crumbs in a tablespoon of dried oregano or basil before using.

2 tablespoons olive oil
1 cup coarse bread crumbs from day-old Italian or
*   French bread*

Salt and freshly ground black pepper to taste

Heat the olive oil in a heavy skillet over medium-high heat. Add the bread crumbs and a pinch of salt. Constantly stirring the crumbs and shaking the pan, fry the crumbs until they are golden brown and crisp, about 10 minutes. Taste for salt and pepper.

Makes 1 cup.

Penne with Roasted Tomatoes and Eggplant

Slowly roasting tomatoes is a great way to enhance flavor, even with not-so-wonderful, out-of-season tomatoes. The results are really fantastic, though, if you use vine-ripened tomatoes at the height of the season. We prefer the exotic flavors of our Mediterranean Sausage with this eggplant and tomato dish, but you could also use our Italian Turkey and Sun-Dried Tomato Sausage (page 22), Southwest Green Chile Sausage (page 20), or Spicy Louisiana Sausage (page 18). You could also use a high quality, store-bought, spicy Italian sausage. If you can't find penne in your neighborhood, use elbow macaroni instead. We prefer to roast eggplant in the oven, rather than sauté it in oil, because the eggplant cooks more evenly and you won't need as much oil.

Roasted Tomatoes (following)
1 large unpeeled eggplant (1 1/2 to 2 pounds), diced
1/4 to 1/2 cup olive oil
Salt and freshly ground black pepper to taste

1 pound Mediterranean Sausage (page 24) or other spicy sausage
12 ounces dried penne or elbow macaroni
1/2 cup freshly grated Parmesan or Romano cheese

Roast the tomatoes and store until ready to use. Preheat the oven to 400°F. In a large bowl, toss the eggplant in 1/4 cup of oil with a sprinkling of salt and pepper. Spread the eggplant on a baking sheet or roasting pan and bake for 10 minutes. Check the eggplant: If pieces seem dry, brush with more oil and stir thoroughly. Bake about 10 minutes more or until all the eggplant pieces are quite soft and beginning to brown. Remove from the oven, set aside, but do not turn off oven.

In a large heavy skillet over medium-high heat, fry the sausage in 2 tablespoons of the olive oil. Leave the sausage in fairly large pieces and cook for 5 minutes, stirring occasionally. Add the roasted tomatoes and eggplant, taste for salt and pepper, and set aside.

Meanwhile cook the pasta in a large pot of lightly salted boiling water until al dente, 10 to 12 minutes, and drain. Mix together the pasta, the sauce, and all but about 2 tablespoons of the cheese. Spoon the pasta into a shallow baking dish, sprinkle the top with the remaining cheese, and bake in the preheated 400°F oven until the cheese is golden brown, about 10 minutes. Serve at once.

Serves 6.

Roasted Tomatoes

Once roasted, the tomatoes can be packed into containers and refrigerated or frozen to be used as a simple and delicious tomato sauce. Covered, they will last in the refrigerator for about a week, frozen for up to three months.

2 pounds Italian-style Roma (plum) tomatoes, each tomato sliced into 2 or 3 thick slices lengthwise
2 tablespoons olive oil
2 tablespoons finely chopped garlic

2 tablespoons chopped fresh herbs (such as basil, oregano, or thyme) or 2 teaspoons dried herbs (use individual herbs or combine)
Salt and freshly ground black pepper

Preheat the oven to 250°F. Spread the sliced tomatoes on baking sheets or roasting pans. Drizzle with olive oil and sprinkle with garlic, herbs, salt, and pepper. Roast until the juices given off by the tomatoes have begun to thicken, about 1 hour. Using a spatula, scrape the tomatoes and all the juices into a nonreactive container. Use at once or cover and store in the refrigerator or freezer until needed.

Makes about 3 cups.

Broccoli Rabe and Sausage with Rotellini and Balsamic Vinegar

Broccoli rabe is a variety of broccoli with smaller heads and a pleasantly bitter flavor. Use it in this recipe or use regular broccoli with heads trimmed and separated into florets (discard thick stalks). Balsamic vinegar—the aged, sweet vinegar made in the northern Italian town of Modena—gives this dish a pleasant sweet/sour character. If you can't find it, use red wine vinegar and add a pinch of sugar or a dash of sweet sherry.

---

1 pound broccoli rabe or broccoli, heads trimmed and
    separated into florets
³/₄ pound dried rotellini, rotelle, fusilli, or other curly pasta
1 tablespoon olive oil
½ pound Italian Turkey and Sun-Dried Tomato Sausage
    (page 22) or good quality Italian sausage
1 medium onion, chopped

1 red bell pepper, seeded, deveined, and chopped
4 cloves garlic, chopped
¼ teaspoon red pepper flakes
¼ cup balsamic vinegar
Salt and freshly ground black pepper to taste
Freshly grated Parmesan cheese for garnish

In a small amount of salted boiling water in a tightly covered saucepan, steam the broccoli rabe or broccoli for 2 to 3 minutes. Be sure not to overcook; the broccoli should be bright green and very crisp. Cool under cold running water, drain, and reserve.

Cook the pasta in a large pot of salted boiling water, while you prepare the rest of the dish. When it is al dente, about 9 to 10 minutes, drain, and reserve.

Heat the oil in a large skillet over medium heat, and fry the sausage for 3 minutes, breaking it up as it cooks. Put in the onion, bell pepper, garlic, and red pepper flakes, and sauté for another 5 minutes, stirring frequently. Add the cooked broccoli rabe or broccoli and the balsamic vinegar, and stir well to mix everything together. Cook for another 3 to 4 minutes, stirring occasionally, until the broccoli is tender, but still crisp. Taste for salt and pepper. Mix the sausage-broccoli mixture with the pasta, sprinkle with Parmesan cheese, and serve hot or at room temperature.

Serves 4 to 6.

Cheese and Sausage Ravioli with Fresh Tomato and Basil Sauce

In many Italian-American households, making ravioli is a complicated, all-day affair, and is usually limited to special occasions and family festivals. But Chinese wonton wrappers, widely available these days, make preparing ravioli a simple task. The wrappers are easy to use, inexpensive, and produce tender and delicious ravioli with a minimum of fuss and mess. We use our Italian Turkey and Sun-Dried Tomato Sausage as a base for the stuffing, but our Mediterranean Sausage (page 24) and Chicken and Apple Sausage (page 16) would also work well.

1 teaspooon olive oil
1/2 pound Italian Turkey and Sun-Dried Tomato Sausage (page 22)
1/2 pound low-fat ricotta cheese

2 tablespoons freshly grated Parmesan cheese, plus more for garnish
25 to 30 square or round wonton wrappers*
Fresh Tomato and Basil Sauce (following)

* See Glossary

In a skillet, heat the olive oil over medium heat and fry the sausage for 4 to 5 minutes, breaking it apart as it cooks. In a bowl, combine the cooked sausage, ricotta and the 2 tablespoons Parmesan cheese and set aside to cool.

Place 1 to 2 teaspoons of the filling in the center of each wonton wrapper, wet the edges, fold into a triangle or half circle, and seal. Cook the ravioli 2 to 3 minutes in a large pot of salted boiling water. Drain and serve with Fresh Tomato and Basil Sauce. Sprinkle with grated Parmesan cheese.

Serves 4 to 6.

Fresh Tomato and Basil Sauce

....

This luscious sauce is best made in late summer or early fall when vine-ripened tomatoes are at their peak. At other times of the year, use high quality canned Italian-style tomatoes. The sauce is delicious on any kind of pasta or over one of our savory waffles (pages 87 to 89). It is also very good served with grilled fish or chicken.

1 tablespoon olive oil
2 teaspoons minced garlic
6 fresh ripe Roma (plum) tomatoes or canned Italian-style
   tomatoes, peeled, seeded, and chopped.

¼ cup chopped fresh basil
Salt and freshly ground black pepper to taste

Heat the olive oil over medium heat in a small nonreactive saucepan and sauté the garlic for 1 minute. Add the tomatoes and cook for 5 more minutes. Put in the basil and cook for 1 minute. Season with salt and pepper, and serve.

Makes 2 cups.

Main Course & Party Dishes

Main Course & Party Dishes

In this chapter we provide recipes that use our sausages in dishes substantial enough to be served as main courses. Some recipes feature sausage patties grilled as a central ingredient with a savory condiment or side dish such as our Asian Mixed Grill (page 156), Braised Sausage with Polenta (page 160), and Chicken and Apple Sausage with Onion Confit (page 148). Others blend sausage into flavorful sauces such as our Swordfish Sicilian Style (page 149), Creole Turkey Grillades (page 169), and Greek Braised Lamb Shanks (page 171).

Sausage adds a delightful undertone of flavor in stews made from a wide range of ingredients like our West L.A. Persian Seafood Stew (page 150), Chicken or Turkey Pozole (page 165), and Greek Sausage and Eggplant Stew (page 172). Stuffings can give richness and an extra flavor to fish and poultry. Edy's Chinese Stuffed Fish (page 152), Stuffed Boned Chicken (page 163), Stuffed Pork Chops with Gorgonzola and Sun-Dried Tomatoes (page 173), and Moroccan Game Hens Stuffed with Rice and Fruit (page 168) are all examples of how sausage enlivens traditional bread and rice stuffings.

Vegetables rise to new heights with sausage in our Chinese Eggplant in Black Bean Sauce (page 162) and Mediterranean Stuffed Peppers (page 188). And old favorites take on new dimensions in Yee Family Tamale Pie (page 180) and Kids' Favorite Chicken and Apple Meat Loaf with Cider Gravy (page 175).

Light and spicy Asian cooking is especially tasty with sausages used to flavor classic dishes such as Thai Green Curry (page 184) and Ken Hom's Mo Shu with Chinese Black Mushroom Sausage (page 186).

Chicken and Apple Sausage with Onion Confit

The sweet-sour onion confit provides a piquant undertone to this mild and lightly sweet sausage and is also delicious with grilled chicken breasts or pork chops. Our Mediterranean Sausage (page 24) works well in this dish, as would good quality, store-bought country sausage. You can also grill the sausage patties as well as panfrying them. This makes a wonderful platter for a special brunch or breakfast or a great main course with mashed potatoes and Cider Gravy (page 176) or baked yams and bitter greens.

2 pounds sweet onions (Vidalia, Maui, or equivalent), halved and very thinly sliced
3 tablespoons olive oil
2 tablespoons balsamic or red wine vinegar

Salt and freshly ground black pepper to taste
1 1/2 pounds Chicken and Apple Sausage (page 16), formed into 8 patties
1 tablespoon vegetable oil for panfrying

In a heavy covered saucepan, cook the onions slowly in the oil and vinegar over low heat until they are soft and almost disintegrating, 35 to 40 minutes. Season with salt and pepper, transfer to a platter, and keep warm.

In a skillet, panfry the sausage patties in the vegetable oil over medium heat, turning frequently, until firm and thoroughly cooked, 5 to 7 minutes. Serve the patties on the bed of onions.

Serves 4.

Swordfish Sicilian Style

The vibrant flavors of Sicilian cooking are found in this spicy dish: garlic, tomatoes, olives, and capers braised with our Mediterranean Sausage and swordfish. It makes a great main course served with large tube pasta such as rigatoni or penne along with a salad of bitter greens, red onions, and oranges. Any leftovers are delicious cold on thick slices of Italian bread or on crostini (page 32). Our Italian Turkey and Sun-Dried Tomato Sausage (page 22) also works well here as would any high quality spicy Italian sausage. Be sure to use European black olives, since most California ripe olives just don't have enough flavor. We prefer Niçoise olives, but dried black Sicilian or Greek Kalamata olives would also be delicious. All of these are high in salt, as are the capers, so be sure to add any salt only after tasting the finished dish.

4 tablespoons olive oil
4 cloves garlic, sliced
1/2 pound Mediterranean Sausage (page 24)
1 can (28 ounces) Italian-style tomatoes, drained
1/4 teaspoon freshly ground black pepper
1/8 teaspoon red pepper flakes or more to taste

1 cup pitted and sliced black olives (French, Italian, or Greek)
1/2 cup capers, rinsed and drained
4 swordfish steaks, 1 inch thick (about 8 ounces each)
1/2 cup chopped fresh parsley
Salt to taste

Heat 2 tablespoons of the olive oil in a large heavy saucepan over medium heat and sauté the garlic until lightly browned, 1 to 2 minutes. Remove the garlic and reserve. Brown the sausage in the pan over medium-high heat, breaking it apart as it cooks, 3 to 4 minutes. Put in the tomatoes, black pepper, and red pepper flakes and cook briskly over high heat for 6 to 8 minutes, crushing the tomatoes with the back of a spoon to thicken the sauce.

In a large skillet with a cover, spread half the tomato sauce and top with half the reserved garlic, 1/2 cup of the olives and 1/4 cup of the capers. Sprinkle with the remaining 2 tablespoons olive oil.

Arrange the swordfish steaks on top of the sauce and cover with the remaining tomato sauce, garlic, olives, capers, and 1/4 cup of the parsley. Cover the pan and simmer until the fish is firm to the touch, 10 to 12 minutes. Taste and add salt *only* if needed. Transfer the swordfish steaks to plates and spoon over them any sauce remaining in the pan. Garnish with remaining parsley.

Serves 4.

West L.A. Persian Seafood Stew

....

BRUCE SAYS:

"WHEN I WAS GROWING UP IN WEST LOS ANGELES (WHICH WE ALWAYS CALLED WEST L.A.), IT SEEMED LIKE EVERY OTHER DAY ANOTHER IRANIAN RESTAURANT WOULD OPEN UP IN THE NEIGHBORHOOD. MANY WERE TINY AND SERVED SPICY HAMBURGERS AND DELICIOUS KABOBS, BUT OTHERS WERE MORE ELABORATE, WITH BIG MENUS IN EXOTIC SCRIPT AND WAITERS IN BAGGY PANTS. I USED TO STOP AND SNIFF THE WONDERFUL SMELLS THAT ISSUED FROM THE KITCHENS WHEN I PASSED BY. AS I GREW OLDER I GRADUATED FROM THE KABOB JOINTS TO THE FANCIER PLACES AND THERE I DISCOVERED THE FANTASTIC FLAVORS OF PERSIAN COOKING. THIS RECIPE IS BASED ON MEMORIES OF ONE OF MY FAVORITE DISHES, WITH HELP FROM MIDDLE EASTERN COOKBOOK AUTHOR CLAUDIA RODEN, WHO SHOWED ME HOW TO MAKE AND USE THE DRIED LIMES THAT FLAVOR MANY MIDDLE EASTERN DISHES."

This dish falls somewhere between a seafood soup and a stew, and makes an excellent first course or light dinner. In place of Middle Eastern dried limes (see Glossary), you can make an infusion of fresh lime peels simmered in water or stock.

4 Middle Eastern dried limes* or peels from 4 fresh limes
2 cups chicken stock, preferably homemade (page 92)
2 tablespoons olive oil
1/4 pound Mediterranean Sausage (page 24)
1 pound monkfish or other firm-fleshed fish, cut into
    1-inch pieces
2 dozen mussels, scrubbed, and beards removed
1/2 pound squid, cleaned and cut into strips (page 122)

1/2 pound scallops
3 medium leeks, trimmed and cleaned with tough green
    parts discarded, coarsely chopped
1 bunch (4 to 6 ounces) cilantro, cleaned and
    coarsely chopped
1/2 cup heavy cream
Salt and freshly ground black pepper to taste
* See Glossary

Simmer dried limes or lime peels in the stock in a covered saucepan to extract the flavor, 1 hour if using dried limes or 30 minutes if using lime peels. Discard limes or peels and reserve the liquid.

Heat the oil in a large heavy pot or Dutch oven over medium heat and fry the sausage for 5 minutes, breaking it up as it cooks. Add the monkfish or other fish chunks and sauté for 5 minutes, stirring occasionally. Add the reserved lime-infused stock and simmer 5 minutes more. Put in the mussels and cook for 2 to 3 minutes. Add the squid and scallops and cook 2 to 3 more minutes, until the mussels open. Remove the seafood and keep warm. Discard any mussels that have not opened.

Pulverize the leeks and cilantro in a food processor or blender or chop very finely, add to the pot, and cook for 5 minutes. Return the seafood to the pot over low heat, stir in the cream, season with salt and pepper to taste, and serve.

Serves 8.

Edy's Chinese Stuffed Fish

As a child of ten, Edy Young, food entrepreneur and master candy maker, was already cooking the family dinner. Her father was a Chinese chef who didn't have the energy to cook after a long day at the stove. He was a demanding, but good, teacher and Edy learned her lessons well. She now owns her own company, Meyh Candy, which produces wonderful candies made from fruit and chocolate. She also prepares sumptuous Chinese banquets and other delicious foods for appreciative friends at her home high up on one of San Francisco's steepest hills.

1 whole sea bass, red snapper, rock cod, or other firm-fleshed fish (1 1/2 to 2 pounds)
1 teaspoon salt
2 tablespoons cornstarch
1/2 pound Chinese Black Mushroom Sausage (page 26)
1/4 cup vegetable oil
1 cup sliced onions
1 tablespoon chopped garlic
3 slices fresh ginger
2 tablespoons soy sauce
1 teaspoon sugar
1/2 cup beer
4 green onions, white and green parts, chopped
Steamed white rice for accompaniment

Slash the fish skin diagonally on both sides at 1- to 1 1/2-inch intervals. Sprinkle with the salt and then dust with the cornstarch. Stuff the interior of the fish with the sausage.

Heat the oil in a skillet large enough to hold the fish and fry the stuffed fish over high heat until golden brown, about 7 minutes per side. Remove the fish carefully and reserve. Pour off all but about 2 tablespoons of the oil in the pan.

Add to the skillet the sliced onions, garlic, and ginger and fry in the oil over medium-high heat until the garlic just begins to brown, about 2 minutes. Return the fish to the pan and pour over it the soy sauce, sugar, and beer. Cover, lower the heat and simmer the fish until the flesh flakes easily when pierced with a fork, about 15 minutes. Add water during cooking if the sauce seems too thick.

Place the whole fish on a serving platter, top with the sauce in the pan, and sprinkle with chopped green onions. Serve with steamed rice.

Serves 4.

Whole Baked Salmon with Oyster and Sausage Stuffing

Baking a salmon or any other large whole fish in a hot oven keeps the flesh moist and delicious. And adding a stuffing made of oysters and aromatic sausage gives the dish an extra dimension. We use a whole salmon here, but almost any large fish such as striped bass, sea bass, red drum or grouper would be delightful. This is a dramatic and beautiful presentation that makes a great centerpiece for a buffet or banquet.

2 tablespoons olive oil
1 whole salmon or other large fish (5 to 6 pounds), cleaned and scaled, with head and tail intact
2 tablespoons fresh lemon juice

Salt and freshly ground black pepper as needed
1/4 pound Spicy Louisiana Sausage (page 18)
Oyster and Sausage Stuffing (following)

Preheat the oven to 425°F. Place a sheet of heavy-duty aluminum foil on a shallow baking pan large enough to hold the salmon (the foil should extend 2 to 3 inches beyond the end of the pan). Spread the foil generously with olive oil and place the salmon in the center. In a small bowl, mix together the lemon juice, 1 teaspoon salt, and 1/2 teaspoon pepper, and rub into the cavity of the fish. Cut 5 or 6 deep slashes (about 1/2 inch deep and 4 inches long) diagonally across the top of the fish. Into each slit insert some of the uncooked sausage. Lightly salt and pepper the fish. Set aside while you make the stuffing.

Carefully place the stuffing in the fish's cavity. It's not necessary to sew up or skewer the cavity, as the stuffing will stay in place during cooking. Put the fish uncovered on the center rack of the oven and bake until the flesh is firm when lightly poked with a finger, 45 to 55 minutes. Use the overlapping foil to lift the fish from the pan and slide it onto a warm platter.

Serves 6 to 8 with leftovers.

Oyster and Sausage Stuffing

....

This rich and savory stuffing is not only delicious in fish, but adds great flavors to chicken or turkey. You can also stuff it into thick pork chops, or serve the dressing as a side dish with grilled or braised pork tenderloins.

2 tablespoons unsalted butter or olive oil
1 cup finely chopped onion
½ cup finely chopped celery
½ cup thinly sliced green onions, white and green parts
1 teaspoon minced garlic
¼ cup chopped fresh mushrooms

½ pound Spicy Louisiana Sausage (page 18)
1 jar (12 ounces) oysters, coarsely chopped, with liquid
2 cups dry bread crumbs or leftover cornbread cut into
  ¼-inch cubes
1 egg

Heat the butter or oil in a heavy 12-inch skillet over medium heat. Add the onions and celery, cover, and cook until onions are soft, about 5 minutes, stirring occasionally. Put in the green onions, garlic, mushrooms, and sausage. Fry uncovered for 5 more minutes, breaking up the sausage as it cooks. Add the oysters and liquid, and cook for 1 minute more. Transfer to a large bowl and mix together with the bread crumbs and egg.

Makes 5 to 6 cups.

The Mixed Grill Goes International: Hold the Mint Sauce, Jeeves!

Grills of various meats served together are found in many cuisines: Southern barbecues with pork and chicken in a fiery sauce; lambs grilled over open fires with spicy sausages at Greek village festivals; sticks of beef and chicken satay grilling on street corners in Bangkok. But the classic mixed grill is found in England and in British-style chop houses in the United States and Canada. The traditional mix is usually lamb or mutton chops, a slice or two of calf's liver or kidney, and a couple of those bland sausages that the Brits are so fond of. This is often served with roasted potatoes, grilled tomatoes, and a mint or parsley sauce.

The English mixed grill is pleasant, but a bit on the stodgy side. With a little imagination—using flavorful marinades, interesting condiments, and some of our sausages—the mixed grill can be transformed into exciting barbecue parties.

Any combination of meats, poultry, sausages, or fish that suits your fancy will work out just fine. We've chosen an Asian motif in the following recipe, but you can probably come up with other themes just as intriguing. Pick out some interesting grilling ingredients that you and your friends like (a mix of seafoods, for example, various sausages, different types of meats and poultry). Make up a flavorful marinade from a culinary tradition you admire (Provençal, Italian, Spanish, Creole). Then match it with one of our sausages (Mediterranean, Italian, Southwest, Louisiana). And don't forget an array of tasty condiments and breads to complement the grills; consult our chart for throwing a Beer and Sausage Tasting Party (page 42). Set out an assortment of salads, fire up the grill, chill down some microbrews, and fall to.

Asian Mixed Grill

You might want to accompany this spicy mixed grill with a flavorful soup like our Chinese Two Cabbage Soup (page 107) or Thai Sausage Soup (page 109) and a pasta dish such as our Singapore Noodles with Black Mushroom Sausage (page 132).

Marinade

2 teaspoons Chinese hot chili paste*
1 tablespoon Chinese brown bean paste*
1 teaspoon Worcestershire sauce
2 tablespoons Asian sesame oil*
2 tablespoons red wine vinegar
2 tablespoons minced garlic
$1/2$ teaspoon five spice powder*
1 tablespoon minced fresh ginger
2 teaspoons sugar
$1/4$ cup soy sauce
2 tablespoons water

For the Grill

6 to 8 chicken legs and/or thighs
6 to 8 small pork chops or country-style spareribs (2 to 3 pounds)
6 to 8 thin slices calf's liver
1 pound Chinese Black Mushroom Sausage (page 26), formed into 6 to 8 patties

Accompaniments

Hoisin Onions (page 218)
Ginger Orange Slaw (page 62)
Mango Vinaigrette (page 219)
Haig's Cilantro Pesto (page 215)

* See Glossary

Mix all the marinade ingredients in a bowl by hand or in a food processor. The marinade should have the consistency of a thick paste. If it seems too thick, add a little more water. Place the meats and liver (not the sausage) on a platter, spread the marinade over them, cover, and marinate 2 hours at room temperature or overnight in the refrigerator.

Prepare a kettle-type barbecue and let the coals burn down to medium-high heat. Grill the chicken legs and thighs with the lid on to make sure the fire doesn't flame up. Turn the chicken pieces often and baste with any leftover marinade. After 15 minutes, add the pork and continue to baste and turn frequently for 10 minutes more. Add the sausage patties and cook about 5 minutes on each side.

Remove pieces of chicken, pork, and sausage to a platter as they are done; chicken should have an internal temperature of 170°F, pork and sausage are done at 160°F. Once all the meats are cooked, keep them warm while you grill the liver with the lid off about 2 minutes on each side. Serve the meats buffet style with suggested condiments and salads.

Serves 6 to 8.

Quick Pizza

Now that we have prebaked pizza crusts like Boboli and others at the local supermarket, you can whip out a tasty pizza any time at all with a little sausage in the freezer, some grated cheese, a few veggies, and a tangy tomato sauce. These quick pizzas can feed the family any night of the week, make great lunches, or can be cut into wedges for delightful appetizers or party snacks. What follows is a basic method for turning out delicious pizzas using our sausages and the time-honored pizza toppings of shredded cheese and tomato sauce. We have added to the basic theme some tasty variations, in which we specify the types of cheese, sausage, sauce, and other toppings. But you should feel free to improvise. Don't limit yourself and your family to Italian ingredients only. Roam the world and your pantry, and let your imagination, your sense of adventure, and the availability of ingredients be your guide.

1 prebaked pizza crust (about 12 inches)
1 cup shredded cheese
½ pound sausage, formed into ½-inch chunks

2 ripe tomatoes, sliced, or ½ cup Fresh Tomato and Basil Sauce (page 145) or other tomato sauce

Preheat the oven to 450°F. Sprinkle the crust with the cheese. Over the cheese, arrange chunks of sausage. Cover this with sliced tomatoes or drizzle with sauce. Add other toppings, if you like, suggested in the following variations. Bake until cheese is melted and the sausage is fully cooked, about 10 minutes. Cut into wedges and serve.

Serves 2 to 3 as a main course, 6 to 8 as an appetizer.

PIZZAPIZZAPIZZA VARIATIONS

Creative chefs are stretching the concept of pizza, turning out crusty pies that are topped with some decidedly exotic ingredients. Wolfgang Puck's caviar-topped pizzas come to mind, along with innovative pizzas using roasted vegetables, black beans, smoked salmon, and even spicy chutneys and various fruits. Remember, you don't have to put tomato sauce and mozzarella cheese on every pizza—you are in charge—have fun and go crazy in the kitchen. What the hell, it's only pizza!

ITALIAN (OF COURSE!):	Italian Turkey and Sun-Dried Tomato Sausage (page 22), mozzarella cheese, thinly sliced fresh mushrooms, Fresh Tomato and Basil Sauce (page 145).
SICILIAN:	Italian Turkey and Sun-Dried Tomato Sausage (page 22), pinch or 2 red pepper flakes, chopped garlic, pitted Sicilian black olives, chopped anchovies, capers, chopped fresh tomatoes.
PROVENÇAL:	Mediterranean Sausage (page 24), sliced tomatoes, fresh goat cheese, chopped fresh oregano, pitted Niçoise olives.
TEX-MEX:	Southwest Green Chile Sausage (page 20), mixture of jack and Cheddar cheese, Salsa Cruda (page 213), fresh corn kernels. Add chopped cilantro after pizza comes out of the oven.
CAJUN:	Spicy Louisiana Sausage (page 18); chopped red onions; small oysters, clams, or shrimp; mozzarella cheese; chopped green onions and garlic; Red Pepper Coulis (page 39), optional. No tomatoes.
ALL-AMERICAN:	Chicken and Apple Sausage (page 16), Sautéed Apple Slices (page 85), sliced sweet onions, mixture of jack and mozzarella cheeses. No tomatoes.
THAI:	Thai Chicken and Turkey Sausage (page 28), chopped red onions, jack cheese, fire-roasted green chiles (page 20), yellow cherry tomato halves. Add chopped fresh mint or basil after pizza comes out of the oven.
CHINESE:	Chinese Black Mushroom Sausage (page 26), sliced bamboo shoots,* chopped green onions, mozzarella cheese, Chinese straw mushrooms.* No tomatoes.

* See Glossary

Braised Sausage with Polenta

This recipe comes from our friend Edy Young, who not only cooks a mean Chinese meal, but turns out some of the best Italian food this side of Tuscany. She made this savory polenta with our Italian Turkey and Sun-Dried Tomato Sausage, but also likes it with our Mediterranean Sausage (page 24) or any good store-bought Italian style sausage.

Polenta (following)
2 tablespoons olive oil
2 pounds Italian Turkey and Sun-Dried Tomato Sausage
   (page 22), formed into 12 patties
1 medium onion, chopped
2 large cloves garlic, minced
2 carrots, chopped

1 celery root, peeled and chopped
2 parsnips, chopped
1 1/2 cups white wine
2 tablespoons tomato paste
Salt and freshly ground black pepper to taste
1 cup chopped fresh basil

Prepare the polenta. While it is cooking, heat the olive oil in a large skillet or Dutch oven over medium heat and fry the sausage patties for 5 minutes on each side. Remove and reserve.

Put the onion and garlic in the skillet and sauté until slightly browned, about 3 minutes. Add the carrots, celery root, and parsnips and then put in the wine and tomato paste. Stir well and bring to a boil. Lower the heat, place the sausage patties carefully on top of the vegetables, cover, and cook gently for about 20 minutes. Taste for salt and pepper.

Transfer the polenta to a large platter or dish, spoon the wine and vegetable mixture over the top, and arrange the sausage patties around the outside of the dish. Sprinkle with the chopped basil.

Serves 6.

Polenta

....

This stick-to-the-ribs staple of northern Italian cooking is widely available in America these days. If you can't find polenta meal in your supermarket or an Italian deli, you can order it easily by mail order (see Sources, page 224). In a pinch, yellow cornmeal could be substituted, but it doesn't work as well. This recipe makes plenty of polenta (we love the leftovers fried or grilled or made into Polenta Croutons, page 117). You could cut the amounts in half if you wanted to serve 4 people with the Braised Sausage.

---

2 cups polenta meal (coarse cornmeal)　　　　　　　*2 teaspoons salt*
2 quarts water

In a large heavy saucepan, mix the polenta and 2 cups of the water. Stir over medium-high heat, gradually adding the salt and the remaining 6 cups water. Bring to a boil and reduce heat to low, stirring constantly until thickened. Cover and cook, stirring occasionally, until the polenta is soft and creamy, 30 to 40 minutes.

Serves 6 to 8.

Chinese Eggplant in Black Bean Sauce

T his is another recipe from Edy Young, a good friend and a great home cook, who was raised in a Chinese-American family that loved hearty food. She grew up learning to cook a great variety of dishes in every style imaginable. She cooks Italian (see Braised Sausage with Polenta, page 160), Mexican (see Yee Family Tamale Pie, page 180), and especially Chinese as we see in this toothsome recipe for spicy eggplant. Edy recommends either our Chinese Black Mushroom Sausage or Thai Chicken and Turkey Sausage for this flavorful dish.

---

1 tablespoon Chinese fermented black beans*
3 tablespoons chopped garlic
¼ cup vegetable oil
1 tablespoon Asian hot chili oil*
³/₄ pound Chinese Black Mushroom Sausage (page 26) or
   Thai Chicken and Turkey Sausage (page 28)
1 cup sliced onions
1¹/₂ pounds small Japanese eggplants, unpeeled, cut into
   2-inch rounds

3 slices fresh ginger
¼ cup beer
2 tablespoons cider vinegar
3 tablespooons brown sugar
¼ teaspoon dried red pepper flakes (optional)
2 green onions, green and white parts, chopped

* See Glossary

Float the black beans in water in a small bowl. Remove the beans with a slotted spoon, leaving any sandy sediment behind. Mash the washed beans in another bowl with the chopped garlic.

Heat the vegetable oil in a wok or large skillet. Fry the black beans and garlic with the chili oil over high heat until the garlic just starts to brown, about 2 minutes. Put in the sausage and sliced onions and stir-fry for 5 minutes, breaking up the sausage as it cooks.

Add the eggplants and ginger along with the beer, vinegar, brown sugar, and dried red pepper flakes, if using. Lower the heat, and simmer until the eggplants are quite tender, about 10 minutes. Spoon into a serving dish and sprinkle with chopped green onions.

Serves 4 as a main course, 6 as part of a multicourse Chinese meal.

Stuffed Boned Chicken

T his sumptuous chicken makes an appealing centerpiece for an elegant picnic or buffet and is delicious roasted or barbecued, hot or cold. An added advantage is that one four-pound chicken will easily feed eight to ten hungry guests, and it is simple to slice and serve. A classic French galantine involves an elaborate presentation of boned poultry stuffed with finely ground meat, liver, and seasoning—essentially a pâté inside a chicken or turkey. Our version is simpler (once the chicken is boned), quicker to make, and, we feel, just as elegant and flavorful. Instead of poaching, the classic technique, we suggest roasting or barbecuing the chicken in a kettle barbecue, which produces a lovely browned bird. Have your butcher bone the bird or bone it yourself. With a little practice it's not as daunting as it sounds.

1 pound Italian Turkey and Sun-Dried Tomato Sausage
   (page 22)
1 cup coarse dry bread crumbs
1/4 cup freshly grated Parmesan cheese
1 box (10 ounces) chopped frozen spinach, defrosted and
   squeezed dry

1 egg
1 roasting chicken (about 4 pounds)
Salt and freshly ground black pepper to taste
2 tablespoons olive oil or more if needed
Mayonnaise or Creole Mustard Sauce (page 207), if
   serving cold

In a large bowl, mix together the sausage, bread crumbs, grated Parmesan, spinach, and egg. Knead the mixture well with your hands or a wooden spoon, and refrigerate while you prepare the chicken.

Preheat the oven to 350°F or light the coals in a covered, kettle-style barbecue prepared for indirect cooking. If you are boning the chicken yourself, place it breast-side down on a cutting board. Using a sharp thin-bladed knife, make a cut all the way down the middle of the back. Insert the blade under the skin and cut against the backbone on either side, pulling up the meat and skin with your fingers as you go. Cut against the ribs and breasts on either side, pulling the meat and skin free. Cut along the thigh bones and pull free the meat and skin as far as the leg joints. Then cut through the leg and wing joints to leave the legs and wings attached. Pull out the carcass (save it for stock), cutting away any meat or skin still adhering to the bones.

(continued on next page)

Place the flattened bird skin-side down and spread the stuffing over the whole inside surface. Reform the chicken to look something like its normal shape, rub with olive oil, and season the skin with salt and pepper. Wrap the chicken tightly in heavy-duty aluminum foil, making sure the breast side is up.

To roast in an oven: Place the chicken in a baking pan and roast for 45 minutes. Cut open the foil, spread it out to expose the skin, and brush the chicken with olive oil. Roast an additional 30 to 40 minutes, until the skin is lightly browned and the internal temperature of the stuffing is 160°F. Let the bird rest for 10 minutes after taking it out of the oven. Remove all the foil, cut off the wings and legs, and slice through the body into $^1/_2$-inch pieces. Arrange slices, wings, and legs on a serving platter.

To cook in a covered barbecue: Spread hot coals around the edge of the prepared barbecue kettle, place a drip pan in the center, and put the foil-wrapped chicken on the grill over the drip pan. Cook for 45 minutes or until the internal temperature of the stuffing is 130°F. Cut open the foil and brush the chicken with olive oil. Continue to roast until the skin is lightly browned, 30 to 40 minutes, and the internal temperature of the stuffing is 160°F. Let the chicken rest for 10 minutes after removing it from the grill. Remove foil, slice, and serve as directed above.

This stuffed chicken is delicious warm, but is also excellent served cold with mayonnaise or Creole Mustard Sauce.

Serves 8 to 10.

Chicken or Turkey Pozole

....

DENIS SAYS:

"THIS IS A REAL FAVORITE IN MY HOUSE, ESPECIALLY WITH MY COLLEGE-AGE KIDS AND THEIR FRIENDS. IT'S BASICALLY POZOLE, THE MEXICAN SOUP/STEW THAT'S USUALLY MADE WITH PORK, HOMINY, AND CHILES, LIGHTENED UP A BIT BY USING CHICKEN OR TURKEY WITH OUR SOUTHWEST GREEN CHILE SAUSAGE. DEPENDING ON HOW MUCH CHICKEN STOCK YOU ADD, IT CAN BE A SOUP, A STEW, OR EVEN A GREAT FILLER FOR BURRITOS. THE KIDS LOVE IT BECAUSE IT'S EASY TO MAKE, DOESN'T CONTAIN A LOT OF MEAT, AND CAN FEED A WHOLE TROOP OF STARVING STUDENTS WITHOUT A LOT OF TROUBLE. THEY HAVE FOUND THAT POZOLE GOES VERY WELL WITH WHATEVER BEER HAPPENS TO BE IN THE REFRIGERATOR AT THE TIME."

1 tablespoon vegetable oil (optional)

1/2 pound Southwest Green Chile Sausage (page 20)

6 chicken thighs or 2 turkey thighs, boned and skinned, cut into 1-inch dice (about 1 1/2 pounds boneless meat)

1 cup chopped onion

1 teaspoon dried oregano

2 tablespoons good quality chile powder*

1/2 teaspoon salt

3 to 4 cups chicken or turkey stock, preferably homemade (page 92)

1/2 cup Salsa Cruda (page 213) or good commercial salsa

1 can (28 ounces) white hominy, drained and washed under cold running water

Salt and freshly ground black pepper to taste

Sour cream or Chipotle Sour Cream (page 212) for garnish

* See Glossary

Heat the oil in a large pot or Dutch oven (if nonstick, eliminate oil) over medium heat and fry the sausage for 3 minutes, breaking it apart as it cooks. Add the chicken or turkey and onion and cook for an additional 2 minutes, stirring well. Put in the oregano, chile powder, salt, stock, salsa, and hominy and simmer over low heat until the chicken or turkey is tender, 20 to 25 minutes. Skim any fat from the top (see Low-Fat Cooking, page 23). Taste for salt and pepper. Serve in soup bowls with sour cream or Chipotle Sour Cream as a garnish.

Serves 4.

Stuffed Turkey Thighs

Not only are these stuffed thighs delicious as a hot main course, but sliced cold with a lemony mayonnaise or our Creole Mustard Sauce (page 207), they make an incredible sandwich or centerpiece for an elegant picnic. Use any spicy fresh sausage here (see pages 18 to 29). Our Spicy Louisiana, Italian Turkey and Sun-Dried Tomato, Mediterranean, Southwest Green Chile, or either Asian sausage work well in this stuffing.

Stuffing
1 pound fresh spinach or 1 package (10 ounces) chopped
  frozen spinach
2 tablespoons olive oil
1 cup finely chopped onions or leeks (white parts only)
1/2 pound spicy sausage
1/2 cup coarse bread crumbs made from day-old bread

1/4 cup freshly grated Parmesan cheese
1 egg

2 turkey thighs (about 14 ounces each)
Salt and freshly ground black pepper to taste
2 tablespoons melted butter or olive oil

To make the stuffing: Rinse the fresh spinach (but do not dry) and place in a covered Dutch oven or deep-sided skillet with no water. Cover and cook over medium heat until wilted, about 2 minutes. Drain and squeeze spinach throughly and chop coarsely. If using frozen chopped spinach, defrost it completely and squeeze it in a strainer to remove any excess liquid.

Heat the oil over medium heat and add the onions or leeks. Cook until soft, stirring frequently, about 5 to 7 minutes. Mix throughly with the spinach, sausage, bread crumbs, cheese, and eggs in a large bowl. Refrigerate the stuffing while preparing the turkey. (The stuffing can be prepared one day ahead and held in the refrigerator; do not stuff turkey, however, until just before cooking.)

To prepare the turkey thighs: Preheat the oven to 350°F. Pat the turkey thighs dry and place each thigh, skin side down, on a work surface. Cut between the thigh bone and meat, using a small sharp knife, and remove the bone. Spoon half of the stuffing into the pocket left by the bone in each thigh. Season the skin with salt and pepper. Wrap each thigh tightly in heavy-duty aluminum foil and arrange them, skin side up and seam side down, in a roasting pan.

Roast the turkey thighs for 45 minutes, then open the foil and brush the thighs with the melted butter or olive oil. Continue cooking until the skin is light brown and the juices run clear when pierced with a knife (about 30 minutes) or until the thighs reach 160°F internal temperature. Remove the thighs from the oven, unwrap them, and let them stand 10 minutes before slicing crosswise. Degrease the pan juices and pass separately. Refrigerated and tightly wrapped, the cooked thighs will keep for 3 days.

Serves 4 to 6.

Moroccan Game Hens Stuffed with Rice and Fruit

hroughout North Africa and the Middle East, you can find poultry cooked in a way that is at the same time exotic and simple: exotic from the use of rare and unusual spices and ingredients such as saffron, pickled or dried lemons and limes, dried fruits, and nuts; simple because the poultry is usually braised in one pot in a highly flavored broth of spices and onions without browning or basting. We've adapted this method to produce braised game hens or small chickens fit for a pasha or at least the neighborhood sultan. The recipe produces quite a bit of sauce that, spooned over couscous or steamed rice, makes a sumptuous side dish.

4 Rock Cornish hens or small chickens (about 1 pound each)
1 recipe Moroccan Rice with Fruit and Almonds (page 203)
1 tablespoon olive oil
2 cups finely chopped onions
2 tablespoons minced garlic
Salt and freshly ground black pepper as needed
1/4 teaspoon ground turmeric

1 tablespoon sweet Hungarian paprika
1 teaspoon ground ginger
1/2 teaspoon ground cumin
Pinch ground cinnamon
3 to 4 cups water
Steamed couscous or rice for accompaniment

Stuff the birds with the rice and fruit mixture and sew or truss the cavity with string or small wooden skewers. Reserve.

Heat the oil over medium heat in a deep-sided skillet with cover or a Dutch oven big enough to hold all 4 birds. Put in the onions, garlic, and a pinch of salt, and cook until the onions are soft, about 10 minutes. Sprinkle 1/2 teaspoon black pepper and the remaining spices over the onions and stir and fry for 1 minute more.

Place the birds on the onions and garlic, breast side up, pour in 3 to 4 cups of water, and bring to a boil. Reduce heat to a simmer, cover, and cook birds for 1 hour, turning them 2 or 3 times while they cook. Remove the birds to a warm platter and keep warm while you reduce the sauce over high heat until it just begins to turn syrupy. Taste for salt and pepper and pour the sauce over the birds. Serve at once with couscous or steamed rice.

Serves 4.

Creole Turkey Grillades

DENIS SAYS:

"THE ORDINARY FLOURISHED IN OAKLAND THROUGHOUT MOST OF THE 1970S AS A RAUCOUS COMBINATION OF CREOLE RESTAURANT, CAJUN ROCKABILLY CABARET, SHOW-PLACE FOR RADICAL THEATER AND POETRY READINGS, AND SOMETIME POOL HALL. I PERFORMED A NUMBER OF FUNCTIONS THERE THAT INCLUDED HEAD WAITER/BOUNCER, MARACAS PLAYER AND BACKUP RHYTHM SECTION, AND FILL-IN COOK WHEN THE KITCHEN STAFF COULDN'T DECIDE WHICH SECTION OF THE UNIVERSE THEY WERE IN THAT NIGHT.

I ALSO COOKED LUNCHES AND PREPPED WHAT SEEMED LIKE TONS OF SHRIMP, RED PEPPERS, GREEN PEPPERS, ONIONS, GARLIC, AND, WORST OF ALL, OKRA, THE SLIME-EEL OF VEGETABLES. ONE OF THE FAVORITE DISHES AMONG THE VARIEGATED CLIENTELE WAS GRILLADES, SPICY SLICES OF BEEF BRAISED IN A PEPPERY SAUCE. WE SERVED IT WITH GRITS AND BIG BOTTLES OF TABASCO, AND IT WAS HIGHLY ESTEEMED BY REVELERS IN THE WEE HOURS AS A WAY TO STRAIGHTEN THEMSELVES OUT FOR THE JOURNEY HOME OR (MORE LIKELY) ON TO THE NEXT PARTY. THIS VERSION USES TURKEY TENDERLOINS OR CUTLETS WITH OUR SPICY LOUISIANA SAUSAGE FOR A LIGHTER, BUT JUST AS FLAVORFUL DISH."

4 tablespoons all-purpose flour
Salt and freshly ground black pepper
1/2 teaspoon paprika
1/8 teaspoon cayenne pepper
1 teaspoon dried oregano
4 turkey fillets, 1/2 inch to 3/4 inch thick (about 1/4 pound each), or 1 pound sliced turkey cutlets
1 tablespoon or more olive oil
1/2 pound Spicy Louisiana Sausage (page 18)
1 cup chopped onion

1 cup chopped, seeded, and deveined red bell pepper
4 cloves garlic, chopped
2 cups canned crushed tomatoes with juice or chopped Italian-style tomatoes
1/2 cup or more chicken stock
2 teaspoons Worcestershire sauce
1/4 teaspoon or more Tabasco
Cooked grits or steamed white rice for accompaniment
Chopped green onions for garnish

Mix together the flour, 1/2 teaspoon salt, 1/4 teaspoon black pepper, paprika, cayenne, and oregano in a small bowl. Place the turkey fillets or cutlets on a plate and rub well with the flour and spices. Set aside the turkey and save any leftover flour and spices.

In a large skillet with cover or in a Dutch oven, heat the oil over medium heat. Brown the sausage for 3 minutes, breaking it apart as it cooks. Remove sausage with a slotted spoon and reserve. In the fat remaining in the pan, brown the turkey fillets or cutlets over medium-high heat, 3 minutes on a side for fillets, 2 minutes on a side for thinner cutlets. Remove and keep warm.

Put the onion, bell peppers, and garlic in the skillet (add a little more oil if needed) and sauté for 3 minutes over medium heat, stirring often.

Stir in the tomatoes, chicken stock, Worcestershire sauce, and Tabasco. Add the reserved sausage and turkey fillets or cutlets. Lower heat to a simmer, cover, and cook until done, 20 to 25 more minutes for the fillets, 10 to 15 minutes for the cutlets. If the sauce seems too thick, add a little more stock; if too thin, remove turkey and reduce sauce over high heat. Taste for salt, pepper, and Tabasco. Serve grillades and sauce over cooked grits or steamed rice and sprinkle with chopped green onions before serving.

Serves 4.

Greek Braised Lamb Shanks

T hese succulent lamb shanks are delicious as a centerpiece for a Greek banquet. Begin with our Mediterranean Seafood and Rice Salad (page 122) and a crisp, nonresinated white wine from Attica (Achaia-Clauss, Demestica). Serve the lamb shanks with a rice pilaf and a Greek country salad of tomatoes, sliced onions, olives, and feta along with a dark red wine from Naoussa in northern Greece.

---

4 lamb shanks (about 1 pound each)
Salt and freshly ground black pepper as needed
1 tablespoon olive oil
¹/₂ pound Mediterranean Sausage (page 24)
1 cup chopped onions
6 cloves garlic, chopped
2 cups canned crushed tomatoes, drained, or chopped
*   Italian-style tomatoes*
1 cup dry red wine

1 cup beef or chicken stock, preferably homemade (page 92)
2 teaspoons dried oregano or 1 tablespoon chopped
*   fresh oregano*
1 teaspoon dried mint or 2 teaspoons chopped fresh mint
1 teaspoon paprika
Pinch ground cinnamon
Chopped fresh parsley for garnish
Cooked pilaf, steamed rice, or lentils for accompaniment

Trim the lamb shanks of any excess fat and sprinkle generously with salt and pepper. In a skillet with cover or a Dutch oven big enough to hold the shanks, heat the oil over medium-high heat. Brown the shanks on all sides, turning often, about 5 minutes. Remove the shanks and keep warm.

   In the fat remaining in the skillet, fry the sausage over medium heat for 3 minutes, breaking it apart as it cooks. Add the onions and garlic and sauté for 3 minutes more. Stir in the tomatoes, wine, stock, oregano, mint, paprika, and cinnamon. Return the shanks to the skillet, bring to a boil, cover, reduce heat, and cook over low heat until the meat is quite tender and almost falling off the bone, 1¹/₄ to 1¹/₂ hours. Turn the shanks after about ¹/₂ hour and check the sauce occasionally; if it is too dry, add a little more wine or stock.

   Remove the shanks with a slotted spoon to a platter. Skim any fat off the surface of the sauce (see Low-Fat Cooking, page 23). If the sauce seems too thin, reduce it over high heat. If too thick, add a little wine or water. Taste the sauce for salt and pepper, spoon it over the shanks, and sprinkle with chopped parsley. Serve with pilaf, steamed rice, or lentils.

Serves 4.

Greek Sausage and Eggplant Stew

*S*petsofai is the Greek version of a hearty sausage stew that is found in virtually all the countries that ring the Mediterranean. What links all these stews is the slow cooking of an assortment of peppers, eggplants, onions, and tomatoes along with sausages of distinct flavor and individual national character. Each sausage variety (*loukanika, merguez, salsicce, saucisse*) provides a unique flavor that distinguishes, for example, the Greek version from the Sicilian, the Spanish from the Dalmatian. Our version of this ubiquitous Mediterranean favorite was adapted from a recipe from Peloponese, the San Francisco Bay Area importer of Greek foods. Serve this rich stew over steamed rice, bulghur wheat, or slices of toasted country bread. It is also delicious with potatoes, panfried or oven-roasted with fresh herbs and garlic. Vary the recipe as you will, using whatever spicy sausage strikes your fancy: Mediterranean (page 24), Italian (page 22), Southwest Green Chile (page 20), or Spicy Louisiana (page 18). Or try a combination of two or three varieties.

---

4 small Japanese eggplants, cut into 1/2-inch rounds
6 tablespoons olive oil
1 pound spicy fresh sausage (see above), formed into 12 equal patties
1 onion, thinly sliced

1 pound vine-ripened tomatoes, peeled, seeded, and chopped
4 bell peppers (green, red, yellow, purple, or in combination), seeded, deveined, and cut into strips
Salt and freshly ground black pepper to taste

Preheat the oven to 400°F. Toss the eggplant slices with 4 tablespoons of the oil in a large bowl to coat the slices well. Spread the eggplant on a baking sheet or baking dish. Bake for 15 minutes and check to make sure the eggplant slices are not too dry; if so, brush with more olive oil. Continue to bake until the eggplant is quite soft, about 10 more minutes. Remove from the oven and reserve.

In a large, heavy, nonreactive saucepan or Dutch oven, heat the remaining 2 tablespoons of olive oil over medium heat and brown the sausage patties for 2 to 3 minutes on each side. Remove from the pan and set aside. Put the onions, tomatoes, and peppers in the pan, and simmer for 15 minutes. Add the eggplant slices and sausage patties and simmer for 15 minutes more. Pour in a little water if the stew seems too dry. Taste for salt and pepper. Serve at once.

Serves 4.

Stuffed Pork Chops with Gorgonzola and Sun-Dried Tomatoes

These piquant chops are great for a special barbecue with a salad of thinly sliced zucchini, red peppers, and chard leaves fresh from the garden. The stuffing also makes a very tasty filling for chicken breasts. You could substitute any good quality Italian sausage or use our Mediterranean Sausage (page 24) or Southwest Green Chile Sausage (page 20). Have your butcher cut pockets into the chops for stuffing or follow the directions below.

4 pork chops (about 1 inch thick)
1 cup coarse bread crumbs from day-old bread
¼ cup pine nuts, toasted lightly (page 113)
2 tablespoons minced sun-dried tomatoes packed in olive oil*
½ pound Gorgonzola cheese, crumbled
1 egg

¼ pound Italian Turkey and Sun-Dried Tomato Sausage (page 22)
2 tablespoons olive oil
Salt and freshly ground black pepper as needed

*See Glossary

Prepare coals in a barbecue for grilling at medium heat. If you are cutting pockets in the chops yourself, lay them flat on a cutting board. Insert a sharp, thin-bladed knife parallel to the table in the middle of the fatty edge of the chop. Push in the knife almost to the bone and cut a pocket in the meat to about ½ inch from one end. Turn the knife and cut to about ½ inch from the other end.

In a large bowl, mix together the bread crumbs, pine nuts, sun-dried tomatoes, cheese, egg, and sausage. Stuff into the pockets of the pork chops and seal with *wooden* toothpicks. Rub the pork chops with the olive oil and season with salt and pepper. Grill over hot coals until firm to the touch, about 10 minutes per side; the meat and stuffing should read 160°F on an instant-read thermometer.

Serves 4.

Meat Loaf: The Ultimate Comfort Food

Meat loaf is everybody's favorite comfort food: After a hectic day, there's nothing like sitting down to a plate of hearty meat loaf, mashed potatoes, and a savory gravy. But too often the meat loaf is bland and uninteresting, and then there's the fat and cholesterol question. Traditional recipes tend to be on the heavy side, with old-fashioned gravy loading up the fat even more.

Using our chicken and turkey sausages combined with either turkey or lean ground beef, you can turn out a great variety of different types of meat loaf with a maximum of flavor and a minimum of fat.

Use the following recipes as guides and improvise with various sausage, spice, and herb combinations.

The basic ratio of 1 pound sausage, $1/2$ pound ground meat, 1 cup bread crumbs, 1 egg, and about $1/2$ cup sauce stays the same. The type of sausage and flavorings can vary as you like.

And what about sauces and gravies? We provide a few recipes and more suggestions, but use your imagination and play around with your favorite recipes. You'll be surprised at how many light and flavorful variations you can come up with.

Be sure to make plenty of meat loaf, as leftovers are never a problem. Think of cold meat loaf as "poor man's pâté," and use it for delicious snacks, appetizers, and sandwiches.

Kid's Favorite Chicken and Apple Meat Loaf with Cider Gravy

This family favorite is a great hit for Sunday dinner with plenty of mashed potatoes, fresh corn, and mugs of root beer. The kids do like a little catsup in the loaf and on the side, but us older folks usually can do without it. And a sweet, amber Oktoberfest lager can replace the root beer in our mugs.

1/2 pound ground turkey or extra-lean ground beef
1 pound Chicken and Apple Sausage (page 16)
1 cup fresh bread crumbs
1 egg
1/4 cup applesauce

1/4 cup catsup (optional for adults, kids love it!)
1 teaspoon Worcestershire sauce
1/2 teaspoon salt
1/4 teaspoon freshly ground black pepper
1 recipe Cider Gravy (following)

Preheat the oven to 350°F. Put all ingredients (except gravy)in a large bowl and mix thoroughly, kneading with your hands, until everything is well blended. Form into a loaf on a baking pan and bake uncovered for 45 minutes to 1 hour. Internal temperature should be 160°F.

To serve, spoon some gravy over slices of meat loaf and serve the rest on the side.

Serves 4 to 6.

Cider Gravy

....

This flavorful gravy is simple to make and can be also be used with roast pork or chops, baked chicken, or ham.

....

1 cup apple cider
½ cup chicken stock
½ cup chopped dried apples

Pinch cinnamon
Salt and freshly ground black pepper to taste
1 tablespoon cornstarch dissolved in ¼ cup apple cider

....

In a nonreactive saucepan, boil down the cider and chicken stock until reduced by ½. Add the dried apples, cinnamon, and salt and pepper to taste. Stir in the dissolved cornstarch and simmer, stirring often, for 5 more minutes before serving. Spoon some gravy over slices of meat loaf, pork, chicken, or ham and serve the rest on the side.

Serves 4 to 6.

Southwest Meat Loaf

This savory meat loaf is great served hot with Lalime's Black Beans (page 196) and Salsa Cruda (page 213). Served cold, it also makes a fantastic filling for Mexican Torta with Lime Pickled Onions (page 59). Try leftovers as filling for tacos or burritos, or crumbled with cheese in a quesadilla.

½ pound ground turkey or extra-lean ground beef
1 pound Southwest Green Chile Sausage (page 20)
1 cup fresh bread crumbs
1 egg

½ cup Salsa Cruda (page 213) or good commercial salsa
½ teaspoon salt
¼ teaspoon freshly ground black pepper

Preheat the oven to 350°F. Put all the ingredients in a large bowl and mix thoroughly, kneading with your hands until everything is well blended. Form into a loaf on a baking pan and bake uncovered for 45 minutes to 1 hour. Internal temperature should read 160°F.

Serves 4 to 6.

Sicilian Meat Loaf

 picy meat loaf just like mama used to make! And this recipe also can turn out really tasty meatballs, too. Just roll them up, brown them in some olive oil, and bake until done (about half an hour) covered with Fresh Tomato and Basil Sauce. Serve meat loaf or meatballs with our Barley and Sausage Risotto (page 200) or Smoked Cheese Polenta with Sun-Dried Tomatoes (page 195).

½ pound ground turkey or extra-lean ground beef

1 pound Italian Turkey Sun-Dried Tomato Sausage (page 22) or other good quality Italian sausage

1 cup fresh bread crumbs

1 egg

½ cup Fresh Tomato and Basil Sauce (page 145) or good quality commercial tomato sauce

¼ cup chopped sun-dried tomatoes packed in olive oil*

2 cloves garlic, chopped

2 tablespoons chopped pitted black olives (preferably dried Sicilian olives)

¼ teaspoon dried red pepper flakes (optional)

½ teaspoon salt

¼ teaspoon freshly ground black pepper

½ cup freshly grated Parmesan cheese

* See Glossary

Preheat the oven to 350°F. Put the meat loaf ingredients, except for ¼ cup of the Parmesan cheese, in a large bowl and mix thoroughly, kneading with your hands, until everything is well blended. Form into a loaf on a baking pan, sprinkle remaining Parmesan over the top, and bake uncovered for 45 minutes to 1 hour. Internal temperature should be 160°F.

Serves 4 to 6.

You can make meat loaf that our grandmas never dreamed of using the preceding methods and the basic proportions of 1 pound sausage, $^1/_2$ pound ground turkey or lean beef, 1 cup bread crumbs, 1 egg, and $^1/_2$ cup sauce, plus other suggested ingredients to taste.

CAJUN MEAT LOAF: Spicy Louisiana Sausage (page 18), chopped red bell pepper, Tabasco, homemade or commercial BBQ sauce.

TERIYAKI MEAT LOAF: Chinese Black Mushroom Sausage (page 26), chopped green onions, homemade or commercial teriyaki sauce.

MEDITERRANEAN
    MEAT LOAF: Mediterranean Sausage (page 24), chopped red bell pepper and green olives, capers, Fresh Tomato and Basil Sauce (page 145) or commercial tomato sauce.

Yee Family Tamale Pie

This spicy casserole is a family favorite in the Yee household, our friend Edy Young's family, where hearty foods from many traditions are enjoyed by everyone from kids to grannies. This tamale pie is easy to make, feeds plenty of people for little money, and, best of all, is absolutely delicious.

Cornmeal crust
1 1/2 cups yellow cornmeal
2 cups cold water
4 cups boiling water
1/2 teaspoon salt
1 stick (1/4 pound) butter, cut into pieces

Filling
2 pounds Southwest Green Chile Sausage (page 20)
1/4 cup chile powder*

1 1/2 teaspoons ground cumin
1 1/2 cups chopped onion
1 small green bell pepper, seeded, deveined, and chopped
2 cups peeled and chopped ripe tomatoes, or canned tomatoes, drained
2 1/2 cups corn kernels (frozen or fresh, removed from cob)
1 cup pitted chopped ripe olives
2 cups shredded Cheddar cheese
Vegetable oil or butter for baking pan
*See Glossary

To make the cornmeal crust: In a bowl, stir together the cornmeal and the 2 cups cold water. In a large saucepan over medium high heat, stir this cornmeal mixture into the 4 cups of boiling water. Add salt, bring back to a boil, and stir in the butter until well blended. Reduce the heat to low, cover, and simmer until the cornmeal is soft and creamy, 30 to 40 minutes, stirring occasionally.

To make the filling: In a large nonstick skillet over medium heat, fry the sausage for 5 minutes, breaking it up as it cooks. Put in all the other ingredients except the cheese and vegetable oil, and sauté until the vegetables begin to soften, about 10 minutes.

To assemble the pie: Preheat the oven to 350°F. Pour 1/2 of the cooked cornmeal into a greased 13x9x2-inch baking pan. Spoon the filling over the cornmeal to 1/2 inch from the edge of the pie. Pour the remaining cornmeal over the filling and smooth the surface with a spatula to seal the edges. Sprinkle with the cheese and bake until golden brown, about 1 hour.

Serves 8.

Stuffed Vegetables

Stuffing vegetables such as tomatoes, peppers, artichokes, and squash with a savory mixture of sausage, bread crumbs, and flavorings is a delicious way to take advantage of the harvest's bounty. Most vegetables are at their best (and cheapest) in late summer, and stuffed vegetables make wonderful summer meals. They are light, but flavorful, and are easy and quick to prepare. With a salad and a crusty loaf of bread, stuffed vegetables make a lovely light dinner, which is inexpensive, nourishing, and low in calories.

For a tasty and unusual appetizer, stuff baby zucchini, pattypan squash, or small tomatoes, and serve warm or at room temperature. Small vegetables will take about one-third less time to cook. Artichokes and eggplants both are delicious stuffed: Use our Creole stuffing (see page 183) for the artichokes and our Italian stuffing (see page 182) for the eggplants.

Use the recipes as guidelines: The basic mixture of 1 pound of sausage to 2 cups of bread crumbs or rice plus 1 egg and seasonings can be varied depending on what vegetables you are stuffing and what flavor accents you desire.

Tomatoes Stuffed with Italian Sausage

These savory stuffed tomatoes are favorites in many Italian-American households. They make a delicious first course or light dinner when accompanied with a substantial salad such as our Italian Sausage and Spinach Salad with Polenta Croutons (page 116). The stuffing also works well with artichokes and eggplants.

8 large ripe tomatoes
1 tablespoon olive oil, plus more for baking
1 pound Italian Turkey and Sun-Dried Tomato Sausage (page 22)
2 cups fresh bread crumbs

1 egg, lightly beaten
2 cloves garlic, chopped
1/4 cup freshly grated Parmesan cheese, plus more for garnish
1/2 teaspoon salt
1/4 teaspoon freshly ground black pepper

Preheat the oven to 350°F. Slice off and discard the stem end of the tomatoes, score the center deeply with a sharp knife, and scoop out the pulp with a soup spoon. You should leave enough to make sure the tomato keeps its shape. Chop and reserve the tomato pulp.

Heat the olive oil in a skillet, and brown the sausage over medium-high heat, breaking it up as it cooks, for 2 to 3 minutes. In a large bowl, mix together the remaining ingredients with the reserved chopped tomato pulp. Add the sausage and any juices from the pan and mix thoroughly.

Stuff the tomatoes with the mixture, packing it fairly tightly. (Any leftover stuffing can be baked in a small pan alongside the tomatoes or used to make meatballs.) Oil a baking pan and arrange the tomatoes in it. Drizzle the top of each tomato with a little olive oil and sprinkle generously with grated Parmesan. Bake uncovered until the tops are lightly browned, 20 to 25 minutes.

Serves 4 as a main course, 8 as a first course.

Creole Stuffed Squash

own in Louisiana they would probably use this stuffing in mirliton (chayote) squash, but it is equally good in zucchini, pattypan, or yellow crookneck squash. You could adapt it to sweeter winter squash such as acorn or butternut by adding a tablespoon or two of brown sugar or sweet sherry to the stuffing. Winter squash will take about one-third longer to cook. This stuffing is also excellent in bell peppers (see Mediterranean Stuffed Peppers, page 184, for cooking directions).

4 medium-sized zucchinis or 8 pattypans (2 to 3 inches in diameter) or other small squash
1 tablespoon olive oil, plus more for baking
1 pound Spicy Louisiana Sausage (page 18)
1 red bell pepper, seeded, deveined, and finely chopped
2 cups fresh bread crumbs

1/2 cup chopped ripe tomatoes
1/2 cup chopped green onions, white and green parts
1 egg, lightly beaten
2 teaspoons Worcestershire sauce
1/2 teaspoon salt
1/4 teaspoon pepper

Preheat the oven to 350°F. Slice the squash in half lengthwise (slice the pattypan through the scalloped edge), score the center deeply with a sharp knife, and scoop out most of the pulp with a teaspoon or melon baller. Leave enough so that the squash will keep their shape. Remove and discard any seeds. Chop pulp and reserve.

Heat the olive oil in a skillet over medium-high heat and brown the sausage, breaking it up as it cooks, for 2 to 3 minutes. Add squash pulp and bell pepper and cook 5 minutes more.

In a large bowl, mix together the remaining ingredients. Add the cooked sausage mixture and any juices in the pan and mix thoroughly.

Stuff the squash liberally with the mixture. Mound the stuffing, packing it in fairly tightly. (Any leftover stuffing can be baked in a small pan alongside the squash or used to make meatballs.) Oil a baking pan and arrange the squash in it, drizzle the tops with oil, and bake uncovered until tops are lightly browned, 20 to 25 minutes.

Serves 4 as a main course, 8 as a first course.

Thai Green Curry

Traditional Thai green curries are made with chicken as in our recipe, but you could also use chunks of boned turkey thighs or lean pork in this zesty dish. If you already have Thai green curry paste and coconut milk in the back of your fridge from earlier recipes, you can throw this dish together in a jiffy. If not, we provide you with a recipe for making your own green curry paste. You can substitute condensed milk for the coconut milk, although the taste will not be quite the same. Serve this tangy curry over steamed rice or boiled rice noodles.

---

1 tablespoon peanut oil

1/2 pound Thai Chicken and Turkey Sausage (page 28), formed into 1-inch meatballs

4 chicken thighs, boned, skinned, and cut into 1-inch pieces

1 small onion, cut into thin shreds

1 tablespoon chopped garlic

1/4 cup Thai green curry paste,* store-bought or homemade (following)

2 cups coconut milk*

1 cup water or chicken stock, preferably homemade (page 92)

1 1/2 tablespoons Southeast Asian fish sauce*

2 teaspoons brown sugar

3 unpeeled Japanese eggplants (6 to 8 ounces each), diced

10 fresh white mushrooms, quartered

1/2 red bell pepper, cut lengthwise into quarters, seeded, deveined, and sliced crosswise into thin strips

Salt and freshly ground black pepper to taste

1/2 cup fresh basil leaves

* See Glossary

In a large pot or Dutch oven, heat the oil over medium-high heat, put in the sausage meatballs, and lightly brown them for about 3 minutes, turning them often to ensure even browning. Add the chicken and cook 2 minutes more, stirring occasionally. Put in the onions and garlic and fry for 3 minutes, stirring often. Add the curry paste, stir to coat everything well, and cook for 2 minutes. Then add the coconut milk, water or chicken stock, fish sauce, and sugar. Bring to a boil, reduce to a simmer, and add the eggplants and mushrooms. Simmer until the eggplant is soft (taste a piece), about 10 minutes.

Put in the red bell pepper slices, taste for salt and pepper, and add a little more curry paste, if desired. Transfer the curry to a serving bowl and sprinkle with basil leaves.

Serves 4 to 6 as a main course, 6 to 8 as part of a multicourse Thai banquet.

Green Curry Paste

....

Hot chiles make this a pretty fiery sauce, so adjust the level to your tastes. And take care not to rub your eyes when handling hot chiles. This paste will keep for one week covered in the refrigerator and can be frozen for up to three months. The recipe was adapted from Nancie McDermott's wonderful book on Thai cooking, *Real Thai*.

1 tablespoon coriander seeds
1/2 teaspoon cumin seeds
3 whole black peppercorns
1 stalk lemongrass*
1 tablespoon chopped cilantro roots or stems
1 teaspoon chopped fresh ginger
1/2 teaspoon grated lime zest

3 cloves garlic
1 shallot
2 tablespoons chopped hot fresh green chiles (Thai kii noo, jalapeño, serrano, or pequin),* stemmed, split, and seeded
1/2 teaspoon salt
* See Glossary

In a small heavy skillet, dry roast the coriander, cumin seeds, and peppercorns over medium heat, continuously shaking and stirring the pan for 2 to 3 minutes until the seeds become lightly darkened and fragrant. Transfer to a mortar and pestle, spice grinder, or blender and grind to a powder.

Trim and discard the dry outer leaves of the lemongrass stalk, the grassy tops, and the roots, leaving a piece of the center about 3 inches long. Cut the lemongrass heart into 1/2-inch pieces. Put them into a food processor or blender along with the pulverized seeds and all the remaining ingredients, and process into a thick paste.

Makes 1/4 to 1/3 cup.

Ken Hom's Mo Shu with Chinese Black Mushroom Sausage

Ken Hom is a Berkeley-based Chinese-American chef who has successfully merged California-style cooking with Asian traditions in what he calls East-West cooking. His many books and his TV show on the BBC have spread the word about this bright new style of cooking that emphazises absolutely fresh ingredients prepared in exciting and creative ways. His recipe for mo shu pork inspired this adaptation which uses our Chinese Black Mushroom Sausage instead of shredded pork or chicken. The delight of this particular rendition is the crunchy texture provided by the vegetables, mushrooms, and Chinese fungi. You could also use our Thai Chicken and Turkey Sausage (page 28) for this dish.

---

2 eggs, beaten

3 tablespoons dark Chinese soy sauce

4 teaspoons Asian sesame oil*

2 tablespoons peanut oil

¼ ounce Chinese dried wood ear fungi*

¼ ounce Chinese dried lily buds*

½ pound Chinese Black Mushroom Sausage (page 26)

1 medium carrot, cut into julienne strips

1 small red or green bell pepper, seeded, deveined, and
   thinly sliced

4 green onions (white and green parts), thinly sliced

3 tablespoons rice wine or dry sherry

4 ounces fresh bean sprouts

10 to 12 Chinese pancakes* or small flour tortillas

About ½ cup hoisin sauce*

* See Glossary

In a small bowl, beat the eggs with 2 teaspoons of the soy sauce and 2 teaspoons of the sesame oil. Heat 1 tablespoon of the peanut oil in a large wok or 12-inch skillet over medium-high heat. Pour the egg mixture over the surface of the pan to form a thin, crêpelike omelet. Cook until the egg sets and transfer to a platter. Cool, roll up, and cut into thin shreds.

Place the wood ear fungus and lily buds in a heatproof bowl and pour boiling water over them; soak until they soften, for at least 30 minutes. Squeeze the excess liquid out of the fungi and lily buds and cut the fungi into thin shreds. Remove the hard ends from the lily buds and discard.

Heat the remaining tablespoon of peanut oil in a wok or large skillet over high heat. Brown the sausage for 3 to 4 minutes, crumbling it as it cooks. Put in the carrots and stir-fry for 2 minutes. Add the reserved fungi and lily buds, and stir-fry for another minute. Put in the bell pepper, green onions and rice wine or sherry, and stir-fry for 1 to 2 minutes more. Finally, add the remaining 2 teaspoons of sesame oil, 2 $1/3$ tablespoons of soy sauce, bean sprouts, and shredded egg, and stir until all the ingredients are well cooked, but still crisp, about 1 minute. Transfer to a serving platter or shallow bowl.

Meanwhile, warm the pancakes or tortillas above boiling water in a covered steamer for 3 to 5 minutes or heat in a microwave. To serve, spread 1 or 2 teaspoons hoisin sauce over the center of each pancake or tortilla, cover with a row of the sausage-vegetable mixture, roll up, and eat.

Serves 6 to 8 as part of a multicourse Chinese meal.

Mediterranean Stuffed Peppers

Stuffed peppers are found all around the Mediterranean from Greece to Provence. They are often served as part of the ritual appetizer platter accompanied with an anise-flavored aperitif like ouzo or pastis or as a first course with a dry white wine. These stuffed peppers also make a delightful dinner with our Mediterranean Orzo Salad (page 119).

4 large red or yellow bell peppers
2 tablespoons olive oil, plus more for baking
1 pound Mediterranean Sausage (page 24)
1 cup chopped onions
4 cloves garlic, chopped
2 cups cooked white rice
½ cup chopped ripe tomatoes

¼ cup chopped pitted black olives (preferably Niçoise)
½ cup chopped fresh parsley
1 egg, lightly beaten
½ teaspoon salt
¼ teaspoon freshly ground black pepper
Freshly grated Asiago or Romano cheese for topping

Preheat the oven to 350°F. Cut the peppers in half lengthwise, scoop out and discard the seeds and membranes.

Heat the olive oil in a skillet, and brown the sausage over medium-high heat, breaking it up as it cooks, for 2 to 3 minutes. Add the onions and cook for 5 more minutes. Put in the garlic and cook for 2 minutes more.

In a large bowl, mix together the remaining ingredients. Add the sausage mixture and any juices in the pan and mix thoroughly.

Stuff the peppers liberally with the mixture. Mound the stuffing, packing it in fairly tightly. (Any leftover stuffing can be baked in a small pan alongside the peppers or made into meatballs.) Oil an 8x8x2-inch baking dish and arrange the peppers upright in it. Pour boiling water into bottom of pan until about 1 inch deep. Cover with aluminum foil, and bake for 20 minutes (10 minutes more if you like your peppers on the soft side). Remove foil and turn up oven to 400°F. Drizzle the tops with olive oil, sprinkle with grated Asiago or Romano, and bake until tops are lightly browned, about 10 minutes.

Serves 4 as a main course, 8 as a first course.

Sausage-Spiked Side Dishes

Sausage-Spiked Side Dishes

Let's face it. Many side dishes—rice, potatoes, barley, even polenta, and all those veggies—can be a bit on the dull side. But our poultry-based sausages give sparkle and extra flavor to bland starches and just about any vegetable without adding a lot of fat and calories.

All you have to do is fry up a small amount of whatever sausage you think will enhance the dish and provide a flavor profile—a signature of a cuisine—along with extra spice and interest. Thus, for example, you can transform green beans into Italian, Thai, Chinese, Mediterranean, Creole, Southwest, or down-home American dishes by lightly steaming the beans, and then quickly sautéing them with a bit of the sausage of your choice. This same technique can enliven a whole array of vegetables like spinach, chard, cabbage, zucchini, lima beans, and so forth. Experiment and have fun with vegetables, for a change.

A plus to many of our side dishes is that they can be turned into an inexpensive main course simply by adding more sausage to the recipe. Put a little more sausage and perhaps some shrimp into Martha's Georgia Red Rice (page 199) and you have Georgia rice pilau. Throw a bit more Chinese Black Mushroom Sausage into our Chinese Sausage and Vegetable Stir-Fry (page 193) and you have a delicious entrée or a part of a multicourse Chinese feast. The same holds true for our Thai Fried Rice (page 198) and Barley and Sausage Risotto (page 200). Just up the amount of sausage and serve a bigger portion to turn a tasty side dish into a one-pot meal.

Collard Greens, Potatoes, and Creole Sausage

ollard greens and other bitter greens, such as mustard, turnip, chard, or kale are especially good with sausage. Lively sausages like our Spicy Louisiana Sausage or Mediterranean Sausage (page 24) provide a piquant counterpoint to the earthy greens.

1 tablespoon olive oil
¼ pound Spicy Louisiana Sausage (page 18)
1 cup chopped red onion
2 cups diced unpeeled red potato

1 pound collard or other greens, tough stems removed and
*   coarsely chopped*
1 cup cold water
Salt and freshly ground black pepper to taste

In a heavy 4-quart saucepan, heat the oil over medium-high heat and add the sausage and onion. Cook until the onion is soft, about 10 minutes, stirring often and breaking up the sausage as it cooks. Add the potatoes, greens, and the water. Cover and cook until the potatoes are tender, about 20 minutes. Taste for salt and pepper and serve.

Serves 4 as a side dish.

Curried Cauliflower

This spicy cauliflower is an excellent accompaniment to roast chicken or barbecued lamb, and can also be a delicious main course. Match it with a hearty lentil purée (*dahl*), Indian flat bread (*naan*) or pita, our Cucumber and Yogurt Sauce (page 216), and a tangy chutney for a delightful Indian banquet.

3 tablespoons peanut oil or vegetable oil
1 large onion, thinly sliced
2 medium carrots, sliced into rounds
4 cloves garlic, chopped
1/2 pound Mediterranean Sausage (page 24)
2 1/2 to 3 pounds cauliflower, separated into florets
2 tablespoons Indian curry paste*

4 fresh or canned tomatoes, peeled, seeded, and chopped
1 cup plain yogurt
Salt and freshly ground black pepper to taste
Dash or more Tabasco (optional)
Steamed rice for accompaniment
Cilantro sprigs for garnish (optional)

* See Glossary

Heat the oil in a large deep-sided skillet or Dutch oven over medium heat. Put in the onion, carrots, and garlic and cook, covered, for 5 minutes. Add the sausage and cook, uncovered, for 2 minutes more, breaking it up as it browns. Put in the cauliflower and curry paste and stir well to mix all the ingredients. Cover and cook over medium heat for about 10 minutes.

Stir the tomatoes and yogurt into the sausage-cauliflower mixture, along with a pinch of salt and pepper. Cover and cook until the cauliflower is quite tender, about 15 minutes. The yogurt will curdle, but that is OK. If the sauce seems a bit watery, remove the solids with a slotted spoon and boil the sauce until it thickens slightly. Put back the solids and cook a minute to rewarm. Taste for salt and pepper. If you'd like a bit more heat, add Tabasco. Serve with rice and, if you like, garnish with cilantro sprigs.

Serves 6 to 8 as a side dish, 4 to 6 as a main course.

Chinese Sausage and Vegetable Stir-Fry

$\mathcal{S}$tir-frying is an ancient Chinese method of stirring and tossing food vigorously in a wok over very high heat for a short time. Vegetables are especially delicious when stir-fried, since they retain their crispness and fresh flavor. Stir-frying is also one of the healthiest methods of cooking, since just a tiny bit of meat, chicken, or seafood flavors a lot of vegetables. Virtually any vegetable can be stir-fried, so don't be afraid to ad lib and come up with your favorite combination. And a large skillet works as well as a wok.

---

3 tablespoons peanut oil or vegetable oil
1 pound fresh green beans, trimmed and cut into 2-inch
   pieces
1/4 cup thinly sliced onion
1 cup diced, seeded, and deveined green bell pepper

1/4 pound Chinese Black Mushroom Sausage (page 26)
1/2 cup chicken stock (page 92) or Chinese Chicken Stock
   (page 108)
2 teaspoons cornstarch dissolved in a little water
Salt and freshly ground black pepper to taste

Heat a large wok or skillet over high heat with 2 tablespoons of the oil. Put in the beans and stir-fry vigorously for 2 minutes. Put in the onions and peppers and stir-fry for 2 more minutes. Taste a bean and, if it is not tender, sprinkle a couple of tablespoons of water over the beans and stir-fry 1 minute more. Transfer the vegetables to a serving bowl.

Add the remaining tablespoon of oil to the pan and heat over high heat for 30 seconds. Put in the sausage and stir-fry for 3 minutes, breaking it up as it cooks. Add the chicken stock and cook for 2 minutes more. Return the vegetables to the wok along with the dissolved cornstarch and stir well until just thickened, about 30 seconds. Taste for salt and pepper and transfer to a serving bowl.

Serves 4 as a side dish.

Middle Eastern Vegetable Pancakes

These little sausage-spiked pancakes are a great way to spice up vegetables and get the family to clean their plates while getting rid of all those raw or cooked veggies that are cluttering up the fridge. The basic technique is simple: Shred 'em, spice 'em, and fry 'em up in a zesty pancake. If you use raw zucchini, crookneck, or pattypan squash, sprinkle the shredded vegetables with salt, let them sit and drain to remove some of the excess water, and then chop. For cooked vegetables, simply chop them. In addition to summer squash, some of our favorite veggies for this dish are raw onions, chard, and bitter or mild greens, or cooked carrots, turnips, cauliflower, and cabbage.

1 tablespoon olive oil
¼ pound Mediterranean Sausage (page 24) or other spicy fresh sausage
¼ cup finely chopped onions
2 cups shredded raw or cooked vegetables
1 tablespoon all-purpose flour

3 eggs, lightly beaten
Pinch salt and freshly ground black pepper
¼ cup vegetable oil
Cucumber and Yogurt Sauce (optional, page 216) for garnish

In a small skillet, heat the olive oil over medium-high heat and add the sausage and onion. Fry, stirring often, for 5 minutes, breaking the sausage apart as it cooks. Transfer to a mixing bowl and stir in the vegetables, flour, eggs, salt, and pepper. Heat the vegetable oil in a large skillet over medium heat. Spoon in the vegetable-egg mixture to make several 3- to 4-inch pancakes. Fry until golden on 1 side, about 5 minutes, and flip. Fry for another 2 to 3 minutes until golden. Serve 2 to 3 pancakes per person, and garnish with Cucumber and Yogurt Sauce, if you like.

Serves 6 as a side dish, 4 as a main course.

Smoked Cheese Polenta with Sun-Dried Tomatoes

This is a particularly good accompaniment to a relatively simple main course such as broiled fish or chicken, grilled chops, or grilled sausages. The polenta also makes a delicious breakfast or brunch with scrambled or poached eggs. You may substitute our Southwest Green Chile Sausage (page 20), Italian Turkey and Sun-Dried Tomato Sausage (page 22), or any other high quality spicy fresh sausage. The key to making wonderful polenta is long slow cooking and frequent stirring. The best polenta to our taste should be creamy and smooth, somewhat like well-made mashed potatoes. Any leftover polenta can be refrigerated and later cut into slices and fried lightly in olive oil as a tasty side dish with scrambled eggs or grilled meats and poultry.

4 tablespoons olive oil
1/4 pound Spicy Louisiana Sausage (page 18)
1/2 cup chopped onions
6 1/2 cups water
1 bay leaf
1 teaspoon salt
2 cups polenta meal (coarse ground cornmeal)

1/2 cup chopped sun-dried tomatoes* (dry packed, not in oil), soaked in water for at least 15 minutes and drained
1 cup freshly grated Asiago or Romano cheese
1 cup freshly shredded smoked cheese (such as smoked mozzarella or smoked Gouda)

*See Glossary

Preheat the oven to 350°F. In a 3- to 4-quart heavy pot, heat 3 tablespoons of the olive oil over medium heat. Put in the sausage and cook for 1 more minute, crumbling it as it browns. Add the onions and cook, stirring occasionally, until golden, 5 to 7 minutes. Put in the water, bay leaf, and salt. Bring to a boil and gradually stir in the polenta. Reduce the heat to low, add the tomatoes and cheese, and continue to stir the polenta until creamy and smooth, about 30 minutes. The polenta is done when it begins to pull away from the side of the pan. Remove the bay leaf.

Brush a 2- to 3-quart baking dish with the remaining tablespoon of olive oil. Almost fill the dish with the polenta and bake for 20 minutes. Spoon out the polenta to serve.

Serves 6 as a side dish or 4 as part of a hearty breakfast.

Lalime's Black Beans

These versatile beans can be used in a great range of dishes from Southwest-style tacos and burritos to soups, salads, and dips. Black beans (also called turtle beans) are available at specialty groceries or by mail order (see Sources, page 224). This recipe comes from Lalime's, the popular Berkeley restaurant that features many Southwest-style dishes using black beans.

Basic Black Beans

4 cups black beans, soaked overnight in cold water to cover
1/2 onion, peeled
1 tablespoon ground cumin
1 tablespoon paprika
2 dried chile peppers* (such as ancho)
2 bay leaves
Salt and freshly ground black pepper to taste

To finish the beans

1 tablespoon olive oil
1 onion, sliced
1 teaspoon chopped garlic
2 red bell peppers, fire-roasted (page 20), peeled, deveined, and sliced
2 tablespoons Haig's Cilantro Pesto (page 215) or 1/4 cup chopped fresh cilantro
1/2 teaspoon puréed chipotle chiles (page 212)
Salt and freshly ground black pepper to taste

* See Glossary

To make basic black beans: Drain the soaked beans, place in a large pot, and cover with cold water. Put in the $^1/_2$ onion, cumin, paprika, chiles, and bay leaves. Bring to a boil, lower the heat, cover, and simmer until the beans are just tender, about 40 minutes. The time will vary, so taste the beans periodically so as not to overcook; they should be tender, but not falling apart. Taste for salt and pepper. At this point, the beans can be used in any recipe calling for cooked black beans. They can also be refrigerated or frozen (see below) for later use. If you want to serve the beans as a side dish or as a filling for tacos or burritos, proceed with the rest of the recipe.

To finish the beans: Strain the cooked beans, reserving the cooking liquid. Remove and discard the onion, bay leaves, and chiles and return the beans to the pot. Heat the olive oil in a large skillet over medium heat. Sauté the sliced onion and garlic in the oil, stirring often, until soft, about 5 minutes. Put in the bell peppers, cilantro pesto or cilantro, chipotle purée, and 3 cups of the cooking liquid from the beans. Bring to a boil, reduce heat, and simmer gently for 15 minutes.

Combine 1 cup of the cooked beans with 1 cup of the liquid from the skillet, and purée in a food processor or blender. Stir the puréed beans and the onion-pepper mixture in the skillet into the pot of cooked beans, and heat gently for 5 minutes over low heat, stirring occasionally. Taste for salt and pepper and serve. Covered, beans will keep up to 5 days in the refrigerator, 3 months in the freezer.

Makes 6 cups beans, serves 6.

Thai Fried Rice

Many of us have memories of the weekly ritual of Saturday night Chinese takeout with the ever-recurring staples of fried rice, egg foo yung, and sweet and sour pork—dishes that have become clichés of Cantonese food. And today we tend to avoid these foods because our memories of them are not particularly exciting. Instead we seek out those regional styles of cooking that have only lately arrived in America: Szechuan, Hunan, Hakka, and the new cuisine of Hong Kong. But recently we've discovered that fried rice can be a lot more than just leftover rice with diced ham and frozen peas. Freshly made fried rice using spicy sausage and lively herbs and sauces can be an enjoyable main course for a lunch or light dinner. Our recipe should be viewed as a basic outline for fried rice. You can add whatever you want: cooked vegetables, bean sprouts, diced cooked chicken or shrimp, and the like. But don't leave out the sausage; it provides much of the flavor and excitement in the dish. We used our Thai Chicken and Turkey Sausage, but you could use our Chinese Black Mushroom Sausage (page 26), or virtually any high quality sausage with plenty of flavor and spice.

---

1 tablespoon peanut oil
½ pound Thai Chicken and Turkey Sausage (page 28)
1 egg, lightly beaten
2 cups cooked long-grain white rice
2 tablespoons Southeast Asian fish sauce*
½ teaspoon sugar
1 teaspoon catsup

1 tablespoon soy sauce
Juice of ½ lime
¼ cup diced tomato
5 fresh mint leaves, freshly chopped
¼ cup chopped green onions, white and green parts

*See Glossary

Heat the oil in a wok or large heavy skillet over high heat. Add the sausage and stir-fry for 3 minutes, breaking it up as it cooks. Stir in the egg and stir-fry for 20 seconds. Put in the rice and stir well, breaking up any clumps. Stir in the fish sauce, sugar, catsup, soy sauce, and lime juice. Stir-fry for 30 seconds. Add the tomato and stir-fry for 30 seconds more. Transfer the fried rice to a platter or serving bowl, garnish with the mint and green onions, and serve.

Serves 4 to 6 as a side dish.

Martha's Georgia Red Rice

I n Georgia, red rice is a family favorite and is usually served with ham or fried chicken as part of the Sunday dinner. Rice is popular all through the South and is found in a great variety of dishes from the pilaus and perloos of the Carolinas to the jambalayas of Louisiana, which this dish resembles. Martha Perry, a San Francisco Bay Area caterer who hails from the deep South, provides a large assortment of salads to upscale stores and delis. We've adapted this recipe from her Georgia Red Rice Salad with Ham, a very popular dish with clients. If you'd like to turn this recipe back into a tangy salad, just combine any leftover red rice with some diced ham, chopped green pepper, parsley, and a red wine vinaigrette. We like the addition of a bit of andouille, a spicy Cajun-style sausage, to provide a smoky undertone (see Sources, page 224). You could also substitute another smoked sausage such as Polish sausage or *linguiça,* or leave out the sausage altogether if you are counting calories.

1 tablespoon olive oil
½ pound Spicy Louisiana Sausage (page 18)
¼ pound andouille or other smoked sausage (optional), diced
2 cups chopped onion
1 cup chopped celery
1 cup chopped, seeded, and deveined green bell pepper

2 cups uncooked long grain white rice
3 cups peeled, seeded, and chopped ripe tomatoes or 3 cups chopped canned Italian-style tomatoes, drained
1 cup tomato juice
Pinch each *sugar, salt, and freshly ground black pepper*

In a large heavy pot with a cover or in a Dutch oven, heat the oil over medium-high heat and fry the sausage, breaking it up as it cooks, for 3 minutes. Add the onion and celery and fry for 7 minutes more, stirring often. Put in the bell pepper and rice, and stir well until the rice is well coated. Add the tomatoes, tomato juice, sugar, salt, and pepper, and stir well. Bring to a boil and reduce heat to a simmer. Cover and cook until the rice is tender, about 20 minutes (if rice seems dry add tomato juice or water toward the end of cooking). Serve at once.

Serves 6 to 8 as a side dish.

Barley and Sausage Risotto

Traditionally in Italy, risotto is made with short-grain rice and a plethora of other savory ingredients: mushrooms, garden vegetables, seafood, sausage, cheese. A well-made risotto should have a creamy texture with the rice still slightly chewy, never mushy. In northeastern Italy, up near what used to be the Yugoslavian border, lies the region of Friuli. The food here is hearty and rustic, more like the food of the province's Austrian and Slovenian neighbors than the rest of Italy. Instead of rice, the *Friulani* make their risotto from barley. This has several advantages for us here in America. Barley is readily available and is much cheaper than the imported arborio rice used in traditional risotto. And it is very difficult to overcook. Barley goes well with strong flavors such as porcini mushrooms, spicy sausages, raddichio, and various dried beans. It is a delicious grain, and you can experiment with a wide range of ingredients in barley risotto, once you've mastered the basic technique. With this hearty risotto, drink one of the region's fruity white wines: Pinot Grigio or Tocai del Friuli.

1 ounce dried porcini mushrooms or ¼ pound fresh
    shiitake mushrooms
3 tablespoons olive oil
2 cups chopped onion
½ pound Italian Turkey and Sun-Dried Tomato Sausage
    (page 22)

2 cups pearl barley, soaked for 1 to 2 hours in cold water to
    cover and drained
7 to 9 cups chicken stock, preferably homemade (page 92)
1 cup freshly grated Parmesan cheese
Salt and freshly ground black pepper to taste

If you are using dried porcini, reconstitute them with boiling water as directed on page 26, reserve soaking liquid, and chop the mushrooms coarsely. If you are using fresh shiitakes, wash them and remove the tough stems; cut the mushrooms into thin strips and set aside.

Heat the oil over medium-high heat in a large deep-sided skillet or Dutch oven. Put in the onions and cook for 5 minutes, stirring often. Add the sausage and fry for 3 more minutes, breaking it up as it cooks. Put in the barley and stir until well coated with the sausage and onion mixture. Stir in the reserved mushroom liquid plus 2 cups of the chicken stock if you are using porcini, 4 cups of stock if you are using fresh shiitakes.

Cover the pot and cook over medium heat until most of the liquid has been absorbed, about 20 minutes, checking the barley occasionally and stirring to make sure it doesn't stick. Stir in 3 more cups of stock and the mushrooms; cover and cook for 20 minutes more, stirring to keep the mixture from sticking. Taste the barley: If it is still too chewy, add 2 more cups of stock and continue to cook, stirring frequently, until the barley is soft and only slightly chewy. There should be enough liquid so that the sauce is creamy. Add more stock or water if needed.

It may take 1 1/4 to 1 1/2 hours to cook the barley, depending on how dry it was to begin with. When the barley is done, stir in the cheese, taste for salt and pepper, and serve at once.

Serves 8 as a side dish, 6 as a first course.

Savory Bread Pudding

 Lighter than a stuffing and easy to prepare ahead of time, this rich and cheesy bread pudding is a welcome side dish for a large holiday meal or any special dinner. Bruce's wife, chef Nancy Oakes, serves it at her San Francisco restaurant, Boulevard, along with pork chops, veal, or roast chicken. Leftovers are no problem, as this savory pudding is even more delicious rewarmed.

½ stick (4 tablespoons) unsalted butter

2 bunches leeks, cleaned and sliced, white part only

1½ pounds Italian Turkey and Sun-Dried Tomato Sausage
(page 22)

½ pound fresh mushrooms, sliced

8 to 10 cups cubed day-old bread

3 cups half-and-half

6 eggs, beaten

1 teaspoon kosher salt

1 teaspoon freshly ground black pepper

½ cup freshly grated Asiago or Romano cheese

Preheat the oven to 350°F. In a large skillet, melt the butter over medium-high heat, and sauté the leeks until soft, about 5 minutes. Add the sausage and cook 5 minutes, breaking it up as it browns. Put in the mushrooms and cook 2 minutes more, stirring well.

In a large bowl, toss together the bread cubes and the sausage-vegetable mixture. In another bowl, whisk together the half-and-half, eggs, salt, pepper, and cheese and stir into the bread mixture. Pour into a greased 9x13-inch baking dish and press down firmly. Allow the pudding to set for 30 minutes before baking. Bake for 1 hour until done.

Serves 10 to 12.

Moroccan Rice with Fruit and Almonds

This pilaf is inspired by the cooking of Morocco where the sweet taste of dried fruit is often combined with rice, meat, and poultry. It makes a wonderful side dish for grilled or roast chicken, duck, or lamb, and is delicious as a stuffing for chicken or game hens (see page 166).

1 tablespoon olive oil, plus more for casserole
1/4 pound Mediterranean Sausage (page 24)
1/2 cup chopped onion
3/4 cup uncooked medium-grain white rice
1 1/4 cups chicken stock, preferably homemade (page 92)
1/4 cup golden raisins
1/4 cup diced pitted prunes
1 cup diced, peeled, and cored apple (preferably Golden Delicious)
1/4 cup toasted almonds (page 113)
1 tablespoon fresh lemon juice
1 egg, beaten lightly
Salt and freshly ground black pepper to taste

Preheat the oven to 350°F if baking in a casserole. Heat the oil in a skillet over medium heat and fry the sausage and onion for 3 minutes, breaking up the sausage as it cooks. Add the rice and stir until it is coated with the mixture. Pour in the chicken stock, bring to a boil, and reduce to a simmer. Cover and cook until the rice is tender and the liquid is absorbed, about 20 minutes. Put the rice in a large bowl, stir in the remaining ingredients, and mix together well. Taste for salt and pepper. Place the rice mixture in an oiled casserole, cover with aluminum foil, and bake for 30 minutes at 350°F. Or lightly stuff 4 to 6 Rock Cornish hens or other small birds and bake as directed on page 166.

Serves 4 as a side dish; stuffs 4 to 6 Rock Cornish hens.

Onion, Sausage, and Apple Stuffing

Not only is this stuffing great for turkey, but it makes an enjoyable side dish for ham, chicken, or duck. For a lighter version, bake the stuffing separately in a casserole. That way, it doesn't pick up juice and fat from the roasting bird. Our Chicken and Apple Sausage makes a delicious, albeit mild, stuffing. For something a bit spicier, use half Chicken and Apple Sausage and half Spicy Louisiana Sausage or just Spicy Louisiana Sausage on its own.

---

2 tablespoons olive oil, plus more for casserole
2 pounds Chicken and Apple Sausage (page 16), Spicy
   Louisiana Sausage (page 18), or a combination of both
2 cups chopped onions
1 cup chopped celery
1 tablespoon dried sage
1/4 cup dry white wine or apple cider

8 to 10 cups dried bread cubes
4 cups peeled, cored, and diced green apples (such as
   Granny Smith)
2 to 3 cups or more chicken stock, preferably homemade
   (page 92)
Salt and freshly ground black pepper to taste

Preheat the oven to 350°F if baking in a casserole. Heat the oil in a large heavy skillet or Dutch oven over medium heat. Put in the sausage and fry for 3 minutes, breaking it up as it cooks. Add the onion, celery, sage, and wine or cider. Cover and cook until the vegetables are soft, stirring occasionally, about 10 minutes. In a large bowl, mix the sausage-vegetable mixture, bread cubes, and apples. Moisten with the stock until the mixture is moist enough to hold together when molded in a large spoon, but not sopping wet. Use more stock if needed. Taste for salt and pepper.

At this point you can either stuff the dressing lightly into a turkey or large chicken and roast it following your favorite recipe. Or you can bake the stuffing separately in an oiled casserole. If you cook it in a casserole, stir in a bit more stock to make up for the liquid the stuffing would absorb in the bird. Cover the casserole and bake for 45 minutes. This recipe yields enough stuffing for 1 medium turkey (14 pounds), 2 large roasting chickens (5 to 6 pounds each), 3 frying chickens (3 to 4 pounds each), or 6 to 8 squabs or quail.

Serves 8 to 10 as a side dish.

Mango

Pesto

Condiments for Sausages

Condiments for Sausages

Condiments are what give life to even the most mundane foods, especially sandwiches and snacks. We still remember the bologna sandwiches of the schoolyard made bearable (barely) with yellow mustard and green relish. Well, we've come a long way from that early experience, creating condiments that embody the flavors of some of the world's most interesting, and spiciest cuisines. Our Chipotle Sour Cream (page 212), Haig's Cilantro Pesto (page 215), Greek Caper Sauce (page 217), and Mango Vinaigrette (page 219) will all enliven even the dullest ingredients—maybe even that bologna sandwich we've been trying to forget all these years.

Creole Mustard Sauce

Steak, ham, or meat loaf sandwiches are all made even tastier with this tangy sauce. It's great on grilled chicken or fish, and on our Louisiana Po'Boy (page 60). Or try it on fried patties of our Spicy Louisiana Sausage (page 18), Italian Turkey and Sun-Dried Tomato Sausage (page 22), or Chicken and Apple Sausage (page 16).

¹/₂ cup Creole mustard* or other coarse-grained mustard
¹/₄ cup mayonnaise
2 teaspoons prepared horseradish
¹/₂ teaspoon Worcestershire sauce

¹/₂ teaspoon Tabasco or to taste
¹/₂ teaspoon freshly ground black pepper

* See Glossary

Mix together all ingredients thoroughly in a bowl. Keeps in a sealed jar in the refrigerator for 1 to 2 weeks.

Makes about ³/₄ cup.

Nancy's Corn Relish

A sweet and piquant condiment that is delicious with our Chicken and Apple Sausage Waffles (page 88), this flavorful relish is also a fine accompaniment to our Spicy Louisiana Sausage (page 18) and Southwest Green Chile Sausage (page 20). For best results, make the relish in late summer or early fall when the corn and peppers are at their sweetest. The recipe was developed by Bruce's wife, Nancy Oakes, chef-owner of San Francisco's Boulevard restaurant. She prefers to roast the corn in the husk in the oven instead of boiling the shucked ears as she feels that this procedure intensifies the corn flavor.

3 large ears fresh corn
1/2 cup finely chopped red onion
1 medium-sized red bell pepper, seeded, deveined,
  and chopped
1/2 cup chopped fresh parsley

Pinch or more sugar
1 tablespoon rice vinegar*
2 tablespoons olive oil
Salt and freshly ground black pepper to taste
* See Glossary

Preheat the oven to 400°F. Place the corn in its husks on a baking pan or roasting dish. Roast for 15 minutes. Let cool for 5 to 10 minutes and remove the husks and silk. Cut the kernels away from the cobs, taking care not to cut into the cob. In a medium bowl, mix together the corn and the remaining ingredients. Taste for salt and pepper and add additional sugar, if you desire. This relish will keep overnight, well covered but is best eaten the same day.

Makes 3 to 4 cups.

Green Tomato and Red Pepper Relish

This tangy relish is a wonderful way to use up green tomatoes left on the vine in the fall. Make up a double or triple batch: The relish keeps for two weeks in the refrigerator and can be frozen for up to a year. The relish is delicious with our Italian Turkey and Sun-Dried Tomato Sausage (page 22), Chicken and Apple Sausage (page 16), Spicy Louisiana Sausage (page 18), and Mediterranean Sausage (page 24). It is also great on grilled chicken or fish and makes a quick and tasty main course when paired with microwaved fillet of halibut or sea bass.

3 tablespoons olive oil
2 red bell peppers, seeded, deveined, and chopped
2 large green tomatoes, seeded and chopped
1 small onion, chopped
2 cloves garlic, chopped

Pinch red pepper flakes
1 tablespoon balsamic vinegar
Pinch sugar
Salt and freshly ground black pepper to taste
2 tablespoons minced fresh basil

In a nonreactive saucepan or skillet, heat the oil over medium heat. Put in the peppers, green tomatoes, and onion and cook 10 minutes, stirring often. Add the garlic, red pepper flakes, vinegar, and sugar. Cook, stirring, for 2 minutes. Taste for salt and pepper. Remove from heat and stir in the basil. Cool before serving.

Makes 1 1/2 to 2 cups.

Roasted Eggplant and Fresh Tomato Vinaigrette

J ust about any sandwich is improved by adding this rich and smoky eggplant relish, but it's especially delicious with our Italian Super Hero (page 56). It is also a perfect addition to an antipasto platter of grilled vegetables and spicy sausage. It goes well with our Italian Turkey and Sun-Dried Tomato Sausage (page 22) and is very tasty with our Mediterranean Sausage (page 24) and Southwest Green Chile Sausage (page 20).

---

1 medium eggplant
1 recipe (about 1 1/2 cups) Fresh Tomato Vinaigrette
   (page 33)

Salt and freshly ground black pepper to taste

Preheat the oven to 400°F. Pierce the eggplant in several places with a skewer or thin knife. Place in a baking dish and roast until the eggplant is quite soft, 20 to 30 minutes. Cool, cut the eggplant in half lengthwise, and scoop out the soft flesh. Chop coarsely, place in a bowl, and mix with the Fresh Tomato Vinaigrette. Taste for salt and pepper. Keeps 3 to 4 days covered in the refrigerator.

Makes about 3 cups.

Guacamole

uacamole is not only a traditional condiment for Mexican dishes such as Lalime's Southwest Green Chile Burritos (page 40), tacos, and beans, but it is also very tasty with grilled Thai Chicken and Turkey Sausage (page 28) and Chinese Black Mushroom Sausage (page 26). It makes a great dip for tortilla chips and is delicious on nachos or as a sauce for grilled or poached fish.

2 large avocados (preferably Hass variety), peeled and pitted
¹/₂ cup Salsa Cruda (page 213) or good commercial salsa
¹/₄ cup chopped fresh cilantro

¹/₄ cup finely chopped onion
Fresh lime juice and salt to taste

In a bowl, using a fork or potato masher, mash avocadoes to a coarse, lumpy texture. Stir in the salsa, cilantro, and onion. Season with lime juice and salt to taste. Use as soon as possible after making to avoid discoloration.

Makes about 2 cups.

Chipotle Sour Cream

C hipotles are ripe, red jalapeño chiles that have been dried and smoked. They have a flavor that is absolutely delicious: smoky, earthy, and hot. We use them in a variety of Mexican dishes where they provide a light smoky undertone and an authoritative bite of heat. At Lalime's restaurant in Berkeley, chef Frances Wilson purées the chiles and mixes them with lemon and sour cream to make a very lively sauce.

1 cup sour cream
Pinch salt

¼ teaspoon lemon juice
1 teaspoon puréed dried or canned chipotle chiles (following)

Mix all the ingredients together thoroughly in a bowl.

Makes about 1 cup.

PURÉED CHIPOTLE CHILES

Canned or dried chipotles are found in Latino specialty stores or from mail order (see Sources, page 224). Canned chipotle chiles work fine in most recipes (we recommend Herdez brand)—just purée them in a blender or food processor before using. If you use the dried chiles, soak them in hot water to cover before puréeing.

Salsa Cruda

Fresh salsa is wonderful on all kinds of Mexican and Southwest dishes, poached or microwaved fish, and grilled chicken, pork or steak. Salsa is a truly versatile sauce, and has surpassed catsup as America's biggest-selling condiment. Try it with our Spicy Louisiana Sausage (page 18), Mediterranean Sausage (page 24), and Thai Chicken and Turkey Sausage (page 28)—not just with the Southwest Green Chile Sausage (page 20). If you can't find fresh Anaheim chiles, use one of the excellent canned versions (Ortega and Herdez are both quite good).

½ cup minced onion, red or yellow
1 jalapeño* or other hot chile, seeded
2 Anaheim* or other mild green chiles, fire-roasted and
   peeled (page 20)
⅔ cup chopped fresh cilantro

1½ cups finely chopped ripe tomato
¼ cup fresh lime or lemon juice
Pinch ground cumin
Salt to taste
* See Glossary

Chop all ingredients by hand or in a food processor and mix together in a serving bowl. Keeps 3 to 5 days covered and refrigerated.

Makes about 2 cups.

Lime Pickled Onions

Quesadillas, Mexican tortas or sandwiches (page 59), and many other Southwest dishes are wonderful with these tangy onions. They are also great on meat loaf sandwiches and with our Southwest Green Chile Sausage (page 20), Spicy Louisiana Sausage (page 18), Mediterranean Sausage (page 24), and Thai Chicken and Turkey Sausage (page 28).

---

1 large red onion, thinly sliced
½ teaspoon salt

Juice of 1 lime (about ¼ cup)

Combine all the ingredients in a small bowl. Cover and marinate at least 3 hours at room temperature or overnight in the refrigerator. Keeps 3 to 4 days refrigerated.

Makes about 1 cup.

Haig's Cilantro Pesto

This recipe from Haig Krikorian of Lalime's restaurant in Berkeley is an exciting and lively variation on traditional basil pesto. It is delicious on grilled fish such as swordfish or tuna and makes an unusual, but very tasty pasta sauce when combined with our Italian Turkey and Sun-Dried Tomato Sausage (page 22) and grated Parmesan cheese. The sauce is also very good with our Southwest Green Chile Sausage (page 20), Mediterranean Sausage (page 24), Thai Chicken and Turkey Sausage (page 28), and Chinese Black Mushroom Sausage (page 26).

....

2 bunches (4 to 6 ounces each) cilantro, washed, dried, and large stalks discarded
1 tablespoon fresh lemon juice
1 teaspoon chopped garlic
1 jalapeño* chile, seeded

1 teaspoon ground cumin
1/2 cup olive oil
Salt and freshly ground black pepper to taste

* See Glossary

....

In a food processor fitted with a metal blade or in a blender, process all the ingredients except the olive oil. With the processor or blender on, pour in the oil in a steady stream until the mixture is smooth. Taste for salt and pepper. Cilantro pesto will keep up to a week covered in the refrigerator and up to 6 months frozen.

Makes about 1 cup.

Cucumber and Yogurt Sauce

Fresh cucumbers and tangy yogurt are very refreshing with hot foods such as our Thai Green Curry (page 184) and Curried Cauliflower (page 192) or spicy salads like our Thai Sausage Salad (page 124). This dill-accented sauce also makes an excellent condiment with our Mediterranean Sausage (page 24) and Spicy Louisiana Sausage (page 18), and is a flavorful addition to grilled fish or chicken.

2 cucumbers, peeled, seeded, and cut into ¹/₂-inch dice
1 clove garlic, minced
1 tablespoon chopped fresh dill or 1 teaspoon dried dill
2 tablespoons or more fresh lemon juice

2 tablespoons chopped fresh mint
2 cups high quality plain whole-milk yogurt
Salt and freshly ground black pepper to taste

Mix all the ingredients together in a bowl. Taste for salt, pepper, and additional lemon juice. The sauce keeps overnight covered in the refrigerator, but should be used up within a day or so.

Makes about 3¹/₂ cups.

Greek Caper Sauce

Try this piquant sauce on grilled tuna or swordfish and on just about any seafood. It's also great on grilled lamb or pork, or tossed with chopped fresh tomatoes, Kalamata olives, and feta cheese in a refreshing Greek salad. The sauce is delicious with our Italian Turkey and Sun-Dried Tomato Sausage (page 22), Mediterranean Sausage (page 24), and Spicy Louisiana Sausage (page 18).

1 teaspoon minced garlic
1 teaspoon salt
1/4 cup fresh lemon juice
1 tablespoon freshly grated lemon zest
2 tablespoons drained capers or more to taste
2 cups olive oil

3 tablespoons freshly ground black pepper
1/4 cup chopped green onions, white and green parts
1/2 cup chopped bottled grape leaves*
1 cup chopped fresh parsley

* See Glossary

Mix together all the ingredients thoroughly in a bowl. Will keep covered in the refrigerator for 1 to 2 weeks.

Makes about 3 cups.

Hoisin Onions

Hoisin sauce is a sweet and pungent Chinese sauce that accompanies many classic dishes such as mo shu pork (see Ken Hom's Mo Shu with Chinese Black Mushroom Sausage, page 186) and Peking duck. Here we combine it with sweet onions, vinegar, and soy to make a sweet-and-sour sauce that provides a piquant accent to our Chinese Black Mushroom Sausage (page 26), Thai Chicken and Turkey Sausage (page 28), and Chicken and Apple Sausage (page 16). Use this delectable condiment on sandwiches, over steamed or microwaved fish, and with grilled pork marinated in soy, garlic, and fresh ginger.

1 large sweet onion (Walla Walla, Maui, or Texas U-238), thinly sliced
½ teaspoon salt
2 tablespoons rice vinegar*

2 tablespoons hoisin sauce*
1 tablespoon mayonnaise
1 teaspoon soy sauce
* See Glossary

Toss the sliced onions in a bowl with the salt and let sit at room temperature for 2 to 3 hours. Pour off and discard any excess liquid. Mix the onions thoroughly with the remaining ingredients. The condiment keeps covered in the refrigerator for 2 to 3 days, improving as it ages.

Makes about 1 cup.

Mango Vinaigrette

A ginger-accented vinaigrette that mixes sweet mango with mint, garlic, and lemons, this is a fine condiment for our Thai Chicken and Turkey Sausage (see Thai Sausage Roll with Mango Vinaigrette, page 55). It is also refreshing served with our Thai Green Curry (page 184) and Curried Cauliflower (page 192).

1 ripe mango, peeled and cut up
1-inch piece fresh ginger, peeled and chopped
Freshly grated zest of 1 lemon
2 cloves garlic
¼ cup packed fresh mint leaves

¼ cup white wine vinegar
⅔ cup vegetable oil
Sriracha Thai sweet chili sauce* to taste
Salt and freshly ground black pepper to taste
*See Glossary

Mix all the ingredients except the chili sauce, salt, and pepper in a food processor or blender and process until smooth. Add a dash or 2 of the chili sauce and taste for salt, pepper, and heat level. Keeps covered in the refrigerator for up to a week.

Makes about 1 ½ cups.

Glossary

An excellent source for information on Chinese, Japanese, Thai, and other Asian foods is *Bruce Cost's Asian Ingredients* (William Morrow, 1988).

Anaheim chiles. See chile peppers.

Ancho chiles. See chile peppers.

Asian hot chili oil. A reddish oil, usually sesame based, infused with hot Asian chiles. Use carefully in dipping sauces and to spice up Asian dishes. Can go rancid, so replace occasionally. Easily found in most markets and Asian specialty stores or by mail order (see Sources, page 224).

Asian peanut oil. When we specify Asian peanut oil we refer to cold pressed, highly flavored peanut oil from Chinese and other Asian producers. This should be used for flavor in salad dressings and dipping sauces. Peanut oil for cooking (e.g. Planters) is neutral in flavor and widely used for frying as it has a very high smoking point. Asian peanut oil can be found in Asian specialty stores or by mail order (see Sources, page 224).

Asian sesame oil. Amber-colored oil pressed from roasted sesame seeds and used to flavor many Chinese and other Asian dishes. Use it sparingly as a seasoning in salad dressings, with vegetables, and in stir-fries for a delightfully nutty flavor. Asian seasame oil is not interchangeable with light sesame oil, which is sometimes used in cooking and has very little flavor. Widely available in most markets and Asian specialty stores or by mail order (see Sources, page 224).

Bamboo shoots. Canned bamboo shoots are used in many Chinese and other Asian dishes. They can be found in most supermarkets in the rapidly expanding Asian sections or in Asian specialty stores. Wash thoroughly before using to get rid of any canned taste.

Chile peppers. Often spelled chili or chilli peppers, especially on Asian labels, chiles originated in the Americas and rapidly spread throughout the world of cooking. The fiery bite of chiles is a essential undertone to the foods of Thailand, parts of China (Szechuan, Hunan), India, and, of course, Mexico and the American Southwest. Fresh chiles range from mild (Anaheim, poblano) to medium hot (jalapeño, New Mexican, serrano) to incandescent and downright dangerous (habanero or Scotch bonnet, pequin, Thai bird pepper, kii noo). Jalapeños are also sold pickled in cans or jars (en escabeche). Commonly used dried chiles are anchos (dried poblanos) and chipotles (red jalapeños that are dried and smoked, sold in bulk or canned). Chiles also are often found in powdered form: Commercial chile powders (see listing) usually contain other flavorings; "varietal" chile powders such as ancho or New Mexican are sold pure. Large (and usually mild) fresh green chiles should be fire-roasted, peeled, and seeded (see page 20) before using. Small (and usually hot) fresh green chiles should be split, and the hot seeds and ribs removed. Dried chiles can be ground into powder, or soaked in hot water and puréed in a blender before use. Chiles can be found in many supermarkets as well as in Latino groceries and specialty stores or by mail order (see Sources, page 224). Care should be taken in handling chiles; use rubber gloves or wash your hands thoroughly after touching hot chiles. Ortega brand canned fire-roasted green chiles are an acceptable substitute for fresh mild chiles.

Chile powder. Commercial chile powders often contain inferior grades of ground chile mixed with cumin, oregano, and other spices. We suggest that you use pure ground chiles such as ancho or New Mexican in most recipes. A good commercial powder that is generally available is Gebhardt Chili Powder.

Chinese brown bean paste. A thick sauce made from fermented soy beans available in cans or jars in most markets, in bulk at Chinese or Asian specialty stores, or by mail order (see Sources, page 224). It is found either with whole beans still intact or ground to a smooth paste. Both versions can be used. Keeps indefinitely if stored in a jar in the refrigerator. Taste for salt levels in recipes.

Chinese dark soy sauce. Deeply colored, strongly flavored sauce made from fermented soy beans. Light Chinese soy sauce and Japanese soy sauce provide less intense flavors. All are available in Asian specialty stores or by mail order (see Sources, page 224).

Chinese dried black mushrooms. Dried mushrooms similar to Japanese shiitakes (see listing) found in Asian specialty shops or by mail order (see Sources, page 224). To reconstitute these and other dried mushrooms, see page 26.

Chinese dried lily buds. Dried buds of yellow day lilies, usually sold in plastic packages in Asian specialty stores or by mail order (see Sources, page 224). To reconstitute, soak the buds in warm water until soft, 20 to 30 minutes.

Chinese dried wood ear fungi. Also called tree ears and cloud ear fungi, these mushrooms grow on dead and rotting trees. They have a pleasant crunchy texture and a mild "woody" taste and can be found in Asian specialty shops or by mail order (see Sources, page 224). To reconstitute, soak the fungi in boiling water for about 30 minutes.

Chinese fermented black beans. Salted and fermented soy beans add a pleasant pungent flavor to a wide range of Chinese dishes. They can be found canned or in plastic packages in Chinese and other Asian specialty stores or by mail

order (see Sources, page 224). Crush beans lightly with a cleaver or chop roughly before using. Taste for salt levels in recipes.

Chinese hot chili paste. Chiles are ground and blended into a wide variety of sauces and pastes throughout Asia. Chinese sauces often blend chiles with fermented soybeans and other flavorings. Be careful with these sauces. Taste for heat and salt levels in recipes. Widely available in markets and Asian specialty stores or by mail order (see Sources, page 224).

Chinese pancakes. Also called mo shu wrappers, these thin pancakes are commonly served with Peking duck and mo shu pork. They can be found fresh or frozen in Asian specialty stores. Small wheat tortillas or unsweetened crêpes can be substituted.

Chinese straw mushrooms. Tiny dried or canned mushrooms from China. To reconstitute the dried mushrooms, soak in warm water until tender. Available in Asian specialty stores or by mail order (see Sources, page 224).

Chinese vermicelli noodles. Thin dried rice noodles sold in Asian specialty stores or by mail order (see Sources, page 224). Soak in warm water until soft before adding to stir-fries or other dishes.

Chipotle chiles. See chile peppers.

Coconut milk. Pressed from the meat of freshly grated coconut, this sweet and flavorful milk is used throughout Southeast Asia. It is available canned in Asian specialty stores or by mail order (see Sources, page 224). Stir or shake well before using.

Creole mustard. Flavorful, coarse-grained mustard from Louisiana. Zatarain's is preferred. Available in specialty food stores or by mail order (see Sources, page 224).

Curry paste. See Indian curry paste and Thai green curry paste.

Dried limes. Dried limes are used throughout the Middle East. They are pulverized in a mortar and used as a seasoning or simmered in water or stock to make an infusion for cooking meat, poultry, or fish. Dried limes are available in Middle Eastern specialty stores or by mail order (see Sources, page 224). For a similar effect, simmer fresh lime peels in water or stock (see West L.A. Persian Seafood Stew, page 150).

Five spice powder. A blend of dried, ground star anise, fennel seed, cinnamon, cloves, Szechuan peppercorns, and often other spices sold in many supermarkets as well as in Chinese and Asian specialty stores or by mail order (see Sources, page 225).

Grape leaves. Canned or packed into jars, grape leaves are often stuffed with cooked rice and/or meat in Greek and Turkish dishes such as dolmades. They can also be used to flavor salads and soups. Available at specialty delicatessens or by mail order (see Sources, page 224).

Green chiles. See chile peppers.

Hoisin sauce. A sweet and spicy soybean-based sauce used in many traditional Chinese dishes. Widely available in markets and Asian specialty stores or by mail order (see Sources, page 225).

Indian curry paste. Indian curry paste is used to flavor Indian curries and other spicy dishes. We prefer Patak brand. It can be purchased in Indian or East Asian specialty stores or by mail order (see Sources, page 224).

Japanese dried shiitake mushrooms. Dried mushrooms similar to Chinese dried black mushrooms (see listing). Widely available in better supermarkets and Asian specialty stores or by mail order (see Sources, page 224). To reconstitute, see page 26.

Lemongrass. A fragrant, lemon-flavored grass used extensively in Southeast Asian cooking. Can be found in Asian specialty stores or by mail order (see Sources, page 224). To prepare, trim and discard outer dry leaves, grassy tops, and roots; use only the tender center part, about 3 inches long.

New Mexican chile powder. Made from dried, ground pure New Mexican chiles. Do not confuse with commercial chile powder which usually includes cumin, oregano, and other flavorings. Substitute ancho or California chile powder, Spanish paprika with a pinch of cayenne, or hot Hungarian paprika. Available in Mexican specialty stores or by mail order (see Sources, page 224).

Oyster sauce. Chinese sauce based on oysters used to flavor a wide variety of dishes. Available in most supermarkets and Asian specialty stores or by mail order (see Sources, page 224). Taste for salt levels in recipes.

Panko. Dried Japanese bread crumbs available from Asian specialty stores or by mail order (see Sources, page 224). If you can't find panko, use dried white bread crumbs.

Pequin chiles. See chile peppers.

Queso fresco. Delicious, mild fresh cheese found in Latino groceries. Substitute teleme, jack or other mild white cheese.

Rice stick noodles. Dried rice noodles similar to Chinese vermicelli noodles (see listing). Available in Asian specialty stores or by mail order (see Sources, page 224). Soak in warm water until soft before using.

Rice vinegar. Also called white rice vinegar, this mildly flavored vinegar is used in Japanese and Chinese sauces, salads, and many other dishes. Widely available in supermarkets and Asian specialty stores or by mail order (see Sources, page 224).

Serrano chiles. See chile peppers.

Southeast Asian fish sauce. Pungent and flavorful sauce made from salted fermented fish and used throughout Southeast Asia. Also called nuoc mam. Often blended with Asian chili sauce and vinegar for dipping sauce. Available in Asian specialty stores or by mail order (see Sources, page 224).

Sriracha Thai sweet chili sauce. Southeast Asian sauce made from chiles, vinegar, and sugar, named after a village in Thailand. Use as a dipping sauce, seasoning, and table condiment. Available in Asian specialty stores and by mail order (see Sources, page 224).

Sun-dried tomatoes. Most of our recipes call for Italian-style Roma (plum) tomatoes salted, dried, and packed in jars in olive oil. Dried tomatoes are also available dry-packed in cellophane or plastic packages. Use the oil-packed tomatoes directly in recipes, soak the dry-packed tomatoes in warm water until soft, 20 to 30 minutes before using. Both are available in Italian delicatessens or by mail order (see Sources, page 224).

Thai chiles. See chile peppers.

Thai chili paste. Southeast Asian condiment made from pureed hot chiles and other seasonings. Available in Asian specialty stores and by mail order (see Sources, page 224).

Thai green curry paste. Spicy Southeast Asian flavoring made with chiles, cilantro, lemongrass, and other seasonings. Used in Thai green curries and other flavorful dishes. We prefer Empress Brand Green Curry Sauce. Available from Asian specialty stores or by mail order (see Sources, page 224). To make your own, see page 185.

Water chestnuts. Widely available canned in supermarkets and also found fresh in Asian groceries. Wash thoroughly before using.

Wonton wrappers. Also called wonton skins, these thin pieces of pasta can be used for the traditional Chinese dumplings or for raviolis and other stuffed pasta dishes. Available square or round and in varying thicknesses (thinner is better for most uses). Can be found in most markets and in Asian specialty stores or by mail order (see Sources, page 224).

Sources

SPECIALTY SAUSAGES

Aidells Sausage Company
1575 Minnesota Street
San Francisco, CA 94107
(415) 285-6660

Williams-Sonoma
P.O. Box 7456
San Francisco, CA 94120
(800) 541-2233
Also European, Asian specialty
foods

Zingerman's
422 Detroit Street
Ann Arbor, MI 48104
(313) 663-3354
Also Italian and European specialty
foods and spices

SAUSAGE CASINGS, SAUSAGE-MAKING EQUIPMENT

Carlson Butcher's Supply
50 Mendell Street #12
San Francisco, CA 94124
(415) 648-2601

The Sausage Maker
26 Military Road
Buffalo, NY 14207
(716) 876-5521

SPECIALTY FOODS

Balducci's
424 Avenue of the Americas
New York, NY 10011
(212) 673-2600
Italian, European

Bette's Diner Products
4240 Hollis Street, Suite 120
Emeryville, CA 94608
(510) 601-6980
Pancake mixes, baking supplies

Cafe Beaujolais Bakery
Box 730
Mendocino, CA 95460
(800) 930-0443
Pancake mixes, baked goods

Chang Kee Jan
838 Grant Avenue
San Francisco, CA 94108
(415) 982-1432
Chinese, Asian

Haig's
642 Clement Street
San Francisco, CA 94118
(415) 752-6283
Greek, Middle Eastern,
Indian, Southeast Asian

Mi Rancho
464 7th Street
Oakland, CA 94607
(510) 451-2393
Mexican, Latino

Paprikás Weiss
1572 Second Avenue
New York, NY 10028
(212) 288-6117
Eastern European, spices

Tokoyo Fish Market
1220 San Pablo Avenue
Berkeley, CA 94706
(510) 524-7243
Japanese, Asian

Tommy Tang Seasonings and Sauces
P.O. Box 46700
Los Angeles, CA 90046
(213) 874-3883
Thai, Southeast Asian, spices

Index

The exact equivalents in the following tables have been rounded for convenience.

US/UK
oz = ounce
lb = pound
in = inch
ft = foot
tbl = tablespoon
fl oz = fluid ounce
qt = quart

Metric
g = gram
kg = kilogram
mm = millimeter
cm = centimeter
ml = milliliter
l = liter

Liquids

US	Metric	UK
2 tbl	30 ml	1 fl oz
1/4 cup	60 ml	2 fl oz
1/3 cup	80 ml	3 fl oz
1/2 cup	125 ml	4 fl oz
2/3 cup	160 ml	5 fl oz
3/4 cup	180 ml	6 fl oz
1 cup	250 ml	8 fl oz
1 1/2 cup	375 ml	12 fl oz
2 cups	500 ml	16 fl oz
4 cups/1qt	1 l	32 fl oz

Weights

US/UK	Metric
1 oz	30 g
2 oz	60 g
3 oz	90 g
4 oz (1/4 lb)	125 g
5 oz (1/3 lb)	155 g
6 oz	185 g
7 oz	220 g
8 oz (1/2 lb)	250 g
10 oz	315 g
12 oz (3/4 lb)	375 g
14 oz	440 g
16 oz (1 lb)	500 g
1 1/2 lb	750 g
2 lb	1 kg
3 lb	1.5 kg

Oven Temperatures

Fahrenheit	Celsius	Gas
250	120	1/2
275	140	1
300	150	2
325	160	3
350	180	4
375	190	5
400	200	6
425	220	7
450	230	8
475	240	9
500	260	10

Length Measures

1/8 in	3 mm
1/4 in	6 mm
1/2 in	12 mm
1 in	2.5 cm
2 in	5 cm
3 in	7.5 cm
4 in	10 cm
5 in	13 cm
6 in	15 cm
7 in	18 cm
8 in	20 cm
9 in	23 cm
10 in	25 cm
11 in	28 cm
12/1 ft	30 cm